Martha to the Rescue

A true story about saving Valerie, the famous chicken

By Janet Gates Bonney

Illustrated by Dawn Peterson

For Book Orders
Janet Gates Bonney
207-725-4388

Anchor Publishing Inc.

945 Harpswell Neck Road

Harpswell. Maine 04079

Book Orders: 1-207-833-5100

www.harpswellanchor.com

*W*hen the angels
were busy,
God sent a dog.

"MARtha…MARtha… Where ARE you? I NEED you!"
In a flash a brown and white bundle of energy came zooming around the corner of the house and skidded into a slippery stop right in front of Miss Janet, almost knocking her over. As Martha looked up, the expression in her eyes, her wagging tail and doggie smile asked, "What's up?"

"The snow's piling up fast and we'd better get the hens back into the coop," said Miss Janet. So in a firm voice she called out, "Chickie, chickie, chick, chick, chick," and here they came, lickety split from all directions, slipping and sliding with wings flapping.

"Okay, Marf, let's go to work and get them back into their pen as quickly as we can!"

Martha, who was half collie, half retriever easily herded the girls past the flower gardens, around the raspberry patch and into the fenced-in pen where they could get inside the henhouse and be safely tucked away. But what was this? One was missing! Where was Number Seven? She hadn't come when called with all the others.

"Oh, no! Martha, Number Seven is the hen in just her pinfeather underwear. Now we'll really have to find her FAST. Come on, Marfy, let's do what you do best. Let's look in the woods first. Before the snow gets any deeper, see if you can find any tracks or pick up her scent. Then we'll split up. You check the barn and the other animals. I'll do the pond and under the red pick-up truck, the Huf'nPuf, and meet you at the front door."

After seeing no sign of Number Seven in the woods, off they went in different directions. Martha began barking and sniffing the ground frantically as Miss Janet went down to the pond to see if the run-away had slid down the icy bank into the freezing water. The duck's soft quacking said that none of the hens had been near the pond all morning for a drink.

Martha gave a quick look-see into the barn, but the barn cats couldn't have cared less and went back to sleep. The bunnies were snug in their five little houses and hadn't had any visitors all morning.

Now the hunt was getting serious. The wind was starting to swirl the snow every which way, and it was getting much colder. First small flakes, but now heavy, fat ones were falling, and it was beginning to get dark. Martha came back covered with snow, having had no success.

Then, just as Miss Janet was going into the house to get a flashlight, Martha dove under the front porch and with much excited tail wagging, she backed out and barked, "Here she is, I found her!"

Miss Janet scrunched down in the snow and, sure enough, there she was next to the house foundation, on her back, eyes closed, not breathing, not moving with her feet straight up in the air. A nearby rake was quickly used to pull her out.

Miss Janet picked her up, whispering, "Poor thing, poor thing," and carried her into the kitchen where she put her gently on the table. "Martha, I think we'd better let her legs thaw out so I can fit her into an old shoe box, and then we can bury her when the snow is all gone in the spring. She'll be safe in the box in the old barn freezer."

After an hour or so of leaving her on the table, Miss Janet went back into the kitchen to check on her frozen friend. Much to Miss Janet's surprise and delight, she found a slight throb on Number Seven's neck and one wing twitched.

"Oh, my word, she's alive!" Miss Janet exclaimed. "Let's get busy FAST and see if we can save her! Oh help!" she said.

All of a sudden Miss Janet knew just what she had to do, which was to ever so slowly warm up the little hen. She filled up a big, red hot water bottle, the one in the shape of a bunny rabbit that her daughter had sent her from England. This done, Miss Janet settled down on the living room couch with first a thick towel, the hot water bottle, and finally the patient on her lap.

Slowly moving the stiff legs back and forth was difficult and didn't do much good. Then the furnace went on. "That's a good idea," Miss Janet said to herself.

"I'll put her on the hot air register for a few minutes. That ought to feel good."

Back again on the couch. There was still no pulse. What to do next? Better try CPR, the way they do on the doctor shows. Four swift and firm thumps of pressure on her chest – one, two, three, four. By prying her still almost frozen little beak a tiny bit apart, Miss Janet breathed some warm air, mouth to beak, down her little hen's throat and over her face. She did this repeatedly for quite a few times, hoping for results.

A few more times and finally a little heartbeat was felt in Number Seven's chest.

"Yes, yes!" By golly, it was working. It wasn't long before the little chest was moving up and down all by itself. And then the dear, little soul opened her eyes, and looking right at Miss Janet, cooed softly as if to say, "Thank you for saving me. I really wanted to keep living here with all my friends."

"You must have a real name now, little girl," Miss Janet told her. "We can't keep calling you Number Seven. You deserve better than that. From now on you will be called 'Valerie,' for your valor, which, of course, means having a strong spirit and being *very brave*."

Martha, who had been watching all this, snuggled up close to Valerie and nuzzled her neck. Valerie responded and said "Thank you" with a soft coo.

"Well, now she has to have a safe place to stay while she recovers and grows some good, winter feathers," Miss Janet told Martha, who was then asked to chicken-sit while she went up into the ghostie room in the attic to find the old baby crib. It needed to be brought down, cleaned up and set up in the living room.

Maybe now would be a good time to explain why Valerie didn't have anything on but her pinfeather underwear. In the fall, all the girls would molt, which meant that they would lose most of their summer feathers and lots and lots of new, thick feathers would grow back to keep them warm through the very cold Maine winter to come. In the spring they would molt again, lose the winter feathers and grow summer feather clothes.

Valerie was very young; this was to be her first winter, and she hadn't quite learned that Mother Nature had wanted her to have a nice feather snowsuit like all the other girls.

But back to our story. The crib was all cleaned up, newspapers were put on the floor and two bowls were placed inside – one for corn, one for fresh water. Then a blanket was partially laid over the top to keep out the drafts. A TV was set on a nearby table, and how Valerie loved watching it! The music was the best, even on the commercials. She would softly coo as though she were trying to sing along.

A week later her feathers were coming in so thick and fast it was time to go back to her friends. All of the hens were so glad to see her, and for hours there was much lively conversation among the clucking girls.

"Where have you been?"

"You've been gone for so long!"

"Do tell us everything!"

Somehow the whole story reached a local newspaper, and then it spread like wildfire all over the world. Miss Janet thought the telephone would never stop ringing! There were letters, too, from far away places—Alaska, Canada, Australia and even Nepal. Miss Janet and Valerie were famous!

The local newspaper, the *Times Record*, sent down a reporter to interview Valerie and a photographer to catch the whole scene. Valerie gave him a quizzical look as if to ask, "And what was the question?"

Valerie was an instant celebrity and was even invited to visit nursing homes to cheer up the old folk. She loved the attention. She had her face washed, her feet washed, and a small roll of paper towels went along with her in the cat carrier, just in case.

Everyone wanted to see her, but her favorite was a seventy-four year old gentleman, who had been a farmer all his life. Valerie even sat on his lap in his wheelchair and presented him with a beautiful, brown egg. Miss Janet guessed that was this dear, little hen's way of saying to the world that "with love and caring, miracles do happen."

The End

Some Interesting Facts About Valerie's Story

After the local newspaper reporter gave Valerie's story to the Associated Press,
it immediately became nationwide, then worldwide, in many kinds of news media.
Countless radio and TV stations, newspapers and magazines around
the world told the story for almost a month.

- Fox TV called.

- Paul Harvey told all about the story.

- Regis and Kathy Lee used it.

- David Brinkley gave a lot of air time to the story during his Sunday morning Washington D.C. show. And when asked in an interview what his favorite story was after his many years of broadcasting, he said it was the one about the chicken in Maine who was brought back to life by CPR.

- Erma Bombeck mentioned Valerie as one of her "end of the year" favorite stories.

- *Down East's* Caskie Stinnett wrote a few nice words in the magazine.

- *Yankee Magazine* sent a reporter and a photographer.

- So did a magazine from Australia.

- *Ripley's Believe It Or Not* wrote about it and printed a caricature of Miss Janet and Valerie in their syndicated newspaper articles.

- In 1998, a film crew came from Hollywood to the farm to do a movie about Valerie's experience.

- In 1999, another film crew was called in from Australia to Hollywood and then to the farm to do part of a documentary for *Public Television (PBS)*, called *The Natural History of the Chicken*. It is still being shown worldwide on a regular basis, and the PBS catalog claims it is one of its best sellers. Miss Janet says she is not sure how many languages have been used, but she does know that the film has been presented with her speaking German, Spanish and the language they speak in Nepal.

- The following is a total (so far) of the places that have written letters or called:

29 states	Hawaii
5 Canadian provinces	South America
Australia	And a call from
Guam	a lady in India!

175 YEARS OF
WALTHAMSTOW HALL

A CELEBRATION

Dedicated to all the girls, staff, parents,
Governors and friends who have played a
part in Walthamstow Hall's rich history.

© Walthamstow Hall School, 2014

First published 2014

ISBN 978-0-9929391-0-6

Published by Walthamstow Hall
Holly Bush Lane, Sevenoaks, Kent TN13 3UL

Author: Heather Evernden
Project Editor: Sally Pelling

Designer: Studio, Baines Design
Printed and bound by: Baines Design, Barley House, Cuffley, Hertfordshire EN6 4RY
www.bainesdesign.co.uk

Picture Acknowledgements
TThe front cover and inside front cover illustrations were commissioned by
Walthamstow Hall in celebration of the school's 175th Anniversary. They are lino cuts
of: the Mulberry tree, Walthamstow, a missionary ship, Sevenoaks and Apple Tree
Cottage by Melvyn Evans (renowned local artist and Walthamstow Hall parent).

Many of the photographs and illustrations included in this book have come from the
Walthamstow Hall Archives. Special thanks to Lindsay White, School Archivist for
sourcing these treasures.

The 'new' Senior School photography on pages 4, 68, 69, 70, 71, 72 and 73 of the
book was taken in 2013 by Nick Ivins.

The 'new' Junior School photography on pages 74 and 75 was taken by Roddy Paine.

The photographs on pages 13 and 16 are reproduced with the kind permission of the
Vestry House Museum, London Borough of Waltham Forest.

Contents

Foreword from the Headmistress

It is with great pleasure that I introduce this latest edition of Walthamstow Hall's rich school history; a story that now spans 175 years.

My thanks to Heather Evernden for the painstaking research in the school Archives which unearthed so much of the school "treasure" that she has brought to life in this edition.

The history relayed with such warmth in these pages also lives outside this volume, enveloping the lives of pupils and teachers today. It is indeed in the very fabric of the school building, from the stone steps of the East staircase, worn smooth by generations of school shoes, to the portraits of my forebears keeping an eagle eye on meal times from their vantage points high up in the Dining Hall. Our history also plays an active part in today's curriculum. Our Third Form (Year 7s) spend some of their very first History lessons in the school Archives, scrutinising old photographs, Drama programmes and past editions of CODA and even trying on old school uniforms. They then use these invaluable source materials to prepare fascinating projects and presentations.

Perhaps though, most importantly of all, is the way in which Walthamstow Hall's history invisibly wraps itself around us in school every day. The long-established school ethos and our strong sense of community have been moulded and refined by the experiences of those who have gone before us. They are embedded in the school's "DNA" and still shape our daily lives, as observed by both the *The Good Schools Guide* and the Independent Schools Inspectorate (ISI) in the reports that they have recently published.

"Pupils' spiritual development is outstanding, nurtured by the school's understated but all-pervasive Christian ethos. Pupils' moral development is very strong. They have a well-developed sense of right and wrong, and show considerable personal integrity and tolerance. The extremely high standards of behaviour stem from the school's ethos."
ISI Inspection Report, December 2013

"When the school was set up it was serious about equipping girls to follow in their parents' footsteps and become missionaries, they needed to be adventurous, resourceful and brave and much of this spirit lives on in the present school."
The Good Schools Guide, 2012

Ours is a unique story, and one which we celebrate with pride and thanksgiving.

Mrs Jill Milner, MA Oxon
Headmistress 2002 – present day

Author's Introduction

A great deal can happen in 175 years! And a short time spent browsing in the Archives of Walthamstow Hall soon convinces you of the truth of that. A school – and especially a school that has provided for boarders in the past – has a rich history. The historian, who tries to recount this story, has to make some difficult decisions. What should be included? Which events were important? How can this story be made vivid for its readers?

In this account I have tried to give a narrative that might be read with ease by a variety of readers, whether they be past or present pupils, members of staff, parents of pupils or some of the many friends of the school. Inevitably that has meant that material has been trimmed, potentially interesting topics omitted, and developments which, in reality, unfolded over years, have been necessarily compressed. But perhaps this way the shape of the story emerges more clearly? I hope so.

I need to acknowledge my significant debt to all those earlier writers who have, in the past, told the story of Walthamstow Hall: Elsie Pike and Constance Curryer, U.K. Moore, Joyce Wilkins, Audrey Third and Anne Evans, Ann Vaughan and the compilers of *The Ship's Log*. Their work has been vital in collating and conserving the detailed information we have about the school's past life.

Most of the material used in this book has been found in the Archives; it has been taken from plans, photos, letters, artefacts, committee minutes, artwork, old uniform, badges… sources too numerous to mention. Several people have worked hard in earlier years to arrange and record this material. One of them, in fact, was Miss Pye-Smith, granddaughter of Mrs Foulger, often thought of as founder of the school. Currently, Lindsay White, assisted by Rosaleen Boardman, is making tremendous strides in creating an Archive that can be used by the girls themselves, in History lessons, for example.

Since new items are added to the store almost weekly, the school's lifestory will, no doubt, need to be retold and retold again, over time. I hope that, in this account, factual errors are few and far between. I have had to take the information in the Archives on trust, recognising that sometimes memories may be incomplete or flawed. However, I have read nothing that does not glow with the sense of affection so many have felt, and do feel, for this school.

You will see that the decision was taken to tell the story up to 1946 in prose and then continue up to the present day, in the form of an illustrated timeline. The events recorded in the timeline are a real mixture of the momentous and the smaller events of each era. Every member of a school community will find different events significant: the opening of a new building is very important to the Headmistress, her staff and pupils, but the ban on eating lollies in uniform is also important to the Lower IV!

You will also quickly spot that only Headmistresses are mentioned by name. This fact by no means suggests a neglect of the huge, incalculable contribution made by countless staff, both teaching and domestic, over the last 175 years. Since a hallmark of all who have served this school seems to be dedication, selflessness and long service, it would be quite invidious to single out specific individuals. However, their influence is everywhere In every picture or account of a meal in the Dining Hall, a school trip, a concert, a sports match, you can read the evidence of the work of *all* the staff who have contributed to the work of the school, since 1838.

Towards the back of this publication you will find some voices of 2013. These little descriptions tell of the everyday life of the school in its Anniversary Year – from the girls' perspective. This log of life in 2013 will be stored in the Archives, along with all those voices that have gone before.

Fashions change, new ways of thinking evolve, but key truths remain unaltered. In her Foreword to the 1938 version of *The Story of Walthamstow Hall* Elsie Pike wrote:

"As we look back… we give thanks for all who, in varying ways, in private or public life, at home or abroad, have translated into daily life the lessons learnt here of love to God and service to Man."

In 2013, there is little to add to those words, except perhaps to say a heartfelt "Amen!"

Heather Evernden
May 2013

Acknowledgements

A book of this nature is very much a team effort, so thanks are due to the many people who gave help in its preparation.

I owe a great debt of thanks to Lindsay White, the School Archivist, for her seemingly tireless work, in locating the huge number of documents, illustrations and artefacts, which have contributed to the research for this book. She has been ably assisted by archivist Rosaleen Boardman.

Over the last 175 years, countless individuals have stored, collated and conserved the thousands of items that form the current Archive and, although they cannot now be thanked, we reflect, with gratitude, on their care for, and pride in, this school. We are glad, however, to be able to publicly thank Walthamstow Hall Old Girls' Association for their generous gifts of funding for the Archive.

Sally Pelling, Head of Marketing, has helped to steer the raw material towards the finished production with energy and optimism.

The staff at the Vestry House Museum and Waltham Forest Archive were very helpful in providing information relating to the school's earliest days and permitted the reproduction of some material in their care.

It has been a pleasure to include contributions from current pupils and my thanks go to them and the teachers who have encouraged them.

Melvyn Evans generously gave permission for his superb artwork to be used as a cover design, for which the school is extremely grateful.

We acknowledge our gratitude to the team at Baines Design for their creativity and attention to detail.

Finally, I would like to record my personal thanks to my husband, Roger, for the many roles he has undertaken in seeing the project on its way: assistant researcher, photographer, proofreader and kind critic.

Heather Evernden

An early view of the school in Hollybush Lane, with gardens all around it

Walthamstow Hall photographed in 175th Anniversary Year, showing the "Hub", student entrance and gallery space built in 2012

Chapter 1: 1838-1851

The beginning - in Walthamstow village.

How long can a good idea survive? A decade? A century? Anyone would be delighted to find that a project she had launched was still going strong, 175 years later.

Mrs Foulger and her group of kindly friends in the leafy village of Walthamstow, would surely have been pleased and amazed that the school and home, which they established from such small beginnings in 1838, has celebrated such a significant anniversary, in 2013. One long-reigning queen, Victoria, came to the throne in 1837, just as the new school was being planned; our own Queen Elizabeth celebrated her Diamond Jubilee as plans for the Walthamstow Hall anniversary celebrations were getting under way!

Good schools for girls were few and far between in the early part of the nineteenth century. Red Maid's School in Bristol was founded in 1634 and the Bar Convent School in York, which began its life in France, finally settled into its present home in 1699. Godolphin School, Salisbury, opened in 1707 and the Clergy Orphan Girls' School, in 1749, both financed by subscriptions. Cowan Bridge, known to us as the prison-like "Lowood", in Charlotte Bronte's *Jane Eyre*, followed in 1823. Other well-known girls' schools in Kent are significantly "younger" than Walthamstow Hall: Kent College was founded in 1886, while Benenden School began in 1923. Most nineteenth century girls' schools owed their existence to one particular person or group, who had a vision, or established a need, and set about fulfilling it.

We should not imagine that these schools were always cosy, or even efficient. An inquiry into the state of female education in 1809 concluded that, in some boarding schools, the sheets were "scarcely changed oftener than every four or five months". Elizabeth Sewell, who went to school on the Isle Wight in 1819 (aged four!) describes in her autobiography the meagre diet, cold, wretched, living conditions and harsh punishments of her schooldays.

Dorothea Foulger (affectionately called Dolly) who is usually thought of as the founder of

Dorothea Foulger: she and a group of friends founded a "Home and School" for the daughters of missionaries in 1838

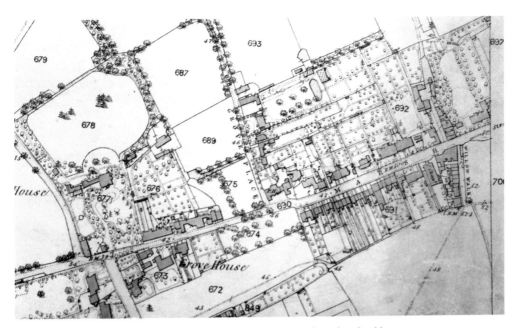

An early map of Walthamstow village, showing Marsh Street, where the school began

Walthamstow Hall School, was married to a Cape merchant and dry-salter, John Foulger. The two had been married in 1811. John was also a Director of the London Missionary Society. Dr Pye-Smith – and that name will recur in this narrative – was another Director of the Society.

Mr and Mrs Foulger lived in a house on Hoe Street, Walthamstow, in a pleasantly rural setting, surrounded by gardens and fields. Their granddaughter, Fanny, recalled their garden: lawns bordered with firs, birch and larch trees, the nearby forest for early-morning rides, the garden pond, "the pear trees and a grand old mulberry, all bearing fruit". Most of all she remembered "the dear people who made life so happy for me and so good for all who came within their influence".

John Foulger was a Deacon of his local Congregational church and, through his work with the London Missionary Society, came into contact with many missionary families. The early Victorian period was a

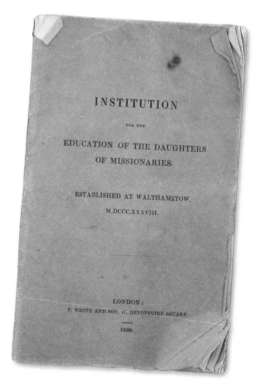

INSTITUTION

FOR THE

EDUCATION OF THE DAUGHTERS
OF MISSIONARIES.

ESTABLISHED AT WALTHAMSTOW.

M.DCCC.XXXVIII.

LONDON:
P. WHITE AND SON, 17, DEVONSHIRE SQUARE.

1839.

The first official "Report of the Institution"

time of intense missionary activity, with the vast reaches of the British Empire providing many places in which to set to work. When missionaries and their wives and children came back to England on leave, many found their way to Hoe Street, to enjoy the hospitality of the generous Foulgers.

The couple must have been made keenly aware of the very difficult circumstances of parents, who felt called to work as missionaries in far-flung countries, and who struggled to provide a suitable education and comfortable home for their children. A school and home for the daughters of missionaries was certainly needed!

In 1838 private schools were opening rather frequently in Walthamstow. In 1820 there were five such schools, including the school that had been attended by Fanny Keats, sister of the poet John Keats. By 1840 there were ten named institutions (often very small) and by 1886 there were thirty-one. Mrs Foulger and her friends were part of a trend!

A meeting to discuss the plight of missionary daughters was held in a schoolroom in Hackney in 1837, after an article had been circulated in the *Evangelical Magazine*. The seed of an idea had been sown! On April 17th 1838, at the house of Mrs Holdsworth, a committee was formed and the school project was set in motion.

A decision to open a school requires funds. Mrs Foulger, Miss Wills, Mrs Reed and Mrs Carey, the group who initiated the project, set to work to find the necessary promises of support. John Foulger gave a donation of £10, Miss Wills gave £25 and promised an annual subscription of £3/3s. Mrs Foulger herself donated £1/1s per year. An appeal went out to many churches and missionary societies to raise subscriptions. Historically, boys' schools have been able to draw upon trusts and legacies, but girls' education has had to look elsewhere for funding.

WALTHAMSTOW MISSION SCHOOL.

An early view of the "Mission School" in Marsh Street, Walthamstow

Hoe Street, Walthamstow, home of Mr & Mrs Foulger

The Reverend Joseph John Freeman had come to be the Pastor of Marsh Street Chapel, in Walthamstow, in 1837. He had worked as a missionary himself, in Madagascar. Reverend Freeman was very supportive of the campaign to provide suitable schooling for missionary children, helping the Walthamstow ladies in raising funds and enlisting supporters.

It became possible, in 1838, to acquire a house situated on Marsh Street, Walthamstow (not far from the Foulgers) and open the new school, with five girls as its first pupils and Miss Wills as the first resident head and "mother" of the institution. A handwritten document in the Archives, which probably dates from the early days of the school's life, tells of the acquisition of the house in Marsh Street. An anonymous lady gave generous help so that a lease on the building could be taken out for an initial period of twenty-one years. After "an outlay of £600 sterling" the house was adapted and spruced up, ready for its new inhabitants. In the school's

early years Mrs Foulger visited the girls and their teachers almost daily.

The 1841 Census tells us who the first school pupils were: Elizabeth Ann Hill, aged ten, and her sister, Mary Mason Hill, aged five, Mary Jane Kidd, aged ten and her sister, Sarah Ann Kidd, aged seven. Another pupil, M.A. Johns, was absent from school when the Census Officers came to call. Their parents were far away in Berhampore, Madagascar and Malacca. Many groups of sisters and cousins went on to attend the school over its long life – and that pattern is still seen today! In the 1850s, seven Drummond girls, all from Samoa, came as pupils. Now, in 2013, we have five pupils, all from the same extended family, which has sent a total of twelve girls to the school, with more still to join in future years!

When Mary Jane Kidd, one of those first five girls, was a very old lady of eighty-two she told Mrs Foulger's granddaughter what she remembered of those very first days of the "home and school". She described the evening of prayer, held on November 16th 1838, when many well-wishers came to pray for a blessing on the girls, their teachers and their life together. She remembered the five wooden stools provided by Mrs Foulger for Mary Jane and her friends to sit on and, most sharply of all, she remembered how she fought to swallow her own tears, as the time came to part from her mother – maybe for years to come. When Mary Jane grew up she became Governess to Mrs Foulger's grandchildren, the Pye-Smiths.

Officially, the school was known as the Institution for the Education of the Daughters of Missionaries, but that was soon shortened, by the general public, to "The Mission School". Nothing of that early school building exists in modern Walthamstow, although a street is named Mission Grove, in memory of the school. The primary school on a site, close to where "The Mission School" originally stood, still carries the name of Mission Grove Primary School. It is said that a mulberry tree was planted in the primary school grounds, to commemorate the mulberry trees once growing in the gardens of Marsh Street. No doubt some of those mulberries had been planted to feed the silkworms kept by families in the silk-weaving trade, like Dorothea Foulger's ancestors, who had fled from France, resettling in England in 1760.

Right from the beginning, the school was described as a "home" for, of course, the girls

The Missionary Mother to her Child.

An illustration from an anthology published to raise funds for missionaries

lived in Walthamstow the whole year round if their parents were stationed somewhere very far away. The public meeting of 1840, which reported on progress, made clear the school's purpose: "That there be provided a comfortable residence, education, board, washing, ordinary medicines and books." The parents were charged £12 per year for under-ten year olds and £15 per year for over-tens. The remainder of the fees was paid by donors. The organising Committee stated that they intended to unite "the comforts and domestic sympathies of home with the order and regularity of school" and hoped to supply "the tender oversight of parents". It certainly sounds more humane than Charlotte Bronte's own schooling.

It is not possible to say who was "Headmistress" in the early days, as the term was not used. There are references to Governesses and Matrons. Mrs Foulger is sometimes referred to as "Cash Secretary" and she continued to be much involved in the important task of fund-raising for the school. It was not until Mrs Cheetham's appointment, in 1859, that anyone held a post rather like a Headmistress of today. Key decisions taken at the outset were that the school should be non-denominational and that the teaching should be Christian, rather than linked to any one particular religious sect or group.

Numbers grew: eighteen girls in 1840, twenty-nine in 1841 (and a waiting list), thirty-seven in 1842, when girls, whose parents were stationed all over the world, were on the roll. They came from Jamaica, Mauritius, India, the East Indies, The Cape of Good Hope and the South Seas. Someone must soon have realised that many of these girls had brothers, who needed similar provision of a "home and school". Thus, in 1842, began the boys' "Mission School", which ultimately became Eltham College, founded by

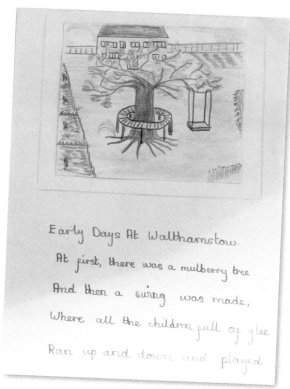

A young pupil's view of the early days in Walthamstow, drawn in 1959

the London Missionary Society and the brother institution to the girls' school. Eltham College moved to its present site, in Mottingham, in 1912.

From the earliest days the symbol of a ship has been very significant for Walthamstow Hall. This description of missionary parents watching their children set sail for school in England, thousands of miles away, was written in 1850:

"Picture the missionary and his wife standing upon the beach. The little boat that is to carry their precious treasures to the vessel, now unfurling her sails to the wind, is about to push off. The moment… of separation is come."

Very soon after the school had been opened, the accommodation began to seem too small. Extensions were built and adjacent property purchased and renovated – just as happens in schools nowadays. The work of the girls was regularly inspected by a Committee and, in 1844, standards were found to be lower than the Inspectors had hoped. Visiting Masters were brought in to teach English, French, German, Arithmetic, Singing, Dancing and Callisthenics (a form of physical training). Quite early in the school's history the girls began to study Latin. It was thought to be a good basis for the study of many languages; it was assumed that many girls would become missionaries when they left Walthamstow and would need to learn the language of the country in which they were stationed. The subjects studied might not form the broad curriculum we would expect nowadays, but it is cheering that those in charge of the school were not content with low standards for girls – by no means always the case in that period.

So the work of the school went on. Accounts of this time recall girls enjoying the peaceful garden with its fruit trees and swing. The girls, we are told, kept silkworms and used the silky threads as bookmarks. The mulberry tree, in the current school grounds in Sevenoaks, may well be a descendant of that Walthamstow mulberry, whose leaves fed those pet silkworms 175 years ago!

A peaceful view of Marsh Street in 1860 when the school was twenty-two years old

Chapter 2: **1851-1878**

The school grows and begins to look for a new home

By the time the Census of 1851 was taken, the school and home at 31, Marsh Street had grown still further. A School Superintendant, two Governesses and an Assistant Governess, a teacher of Music, a Nurse and various domestic staff looked after forty girls. Additionally, the charitable benefactors of the school were also much involved in its affairs.

Mrs Foulger died in 1852, fourteen years after she and other friends had opened the school. Her granddaughter, Fanny, wrote in 1889 that "Mrs Foulger and Miss Wills were indeed mothers at the school". We must be glad they were like "mothers", as some girls at the school were very young indeed to be away from home for years on end. In 1851 the youngest pupil was aged six, but there are records, at other times, of pupils as young as four years old, coming to live at the school. Often several sisters from the same family would all be admitted to the "Mission School" at the same time; it was too difficult and expensive for parents, accompanying their daughters on the long voyage to England, to make the journey very often. Imagine the sudden silence that would fall on those missionary homes as all the children suddenly left.

In those days of devastating illnesses, with no antibiotics available, parents sending their children to school could not be sure they would ever see them again. A father, working as a missionary in "the Americas", wrote in 1847:

"In sending my children home it is nearly the same as to my feelings as burying them: I shall never see them again on this earth."

In 1859 school life changed. Mrs Rebecca Cheetham was appointed to take over all the educational arrangements of the school. A widow, and a clergyman's daughter, she acted more like a modern Headmistress than any of her predecessors. Some of her pupils described her "constant kindness", "firm and gentle authority" and "affectionate sympathy". The girls lived a simple life, by modern standards, but there were treats and outings too: lectures, concerts, magic lantern shows, picnics, visits to exhibitions and galleries.

An important development in girls' education took place in 1867, which saw the completion of the *School's Inquiry Commission*, and its report on the state of education for girls, throughout the nation. The report made clear that girls should be taken as seriously as their brothers, in terms of education, which was not generally the case at the time. A witness to the Commission explained what he thought was the root of the problem:

"The capital defects of the teachers of girls are these: they have not themselves been well taught and they do not know how to teach. Both these defects are accidental and may be remedied."

And remedied they were, for soon there were initiatives to provide teacher training opportunities, at least for those aspiring teachers who lived close enough to a training institution.

The "Mission School" must have been doing rather well by its pupils in its first forty years, if

Miss Unwin and her pupils in Walthamstow in 1879

the careers taken up by its former students are anything to go by. In her book *The Best Type of Girl*, Gillian Avery comments:

"Indeed, in the mid-Victorian period, Walthamstow Hall must have led all the other charitable foundations, if not most girls' schools, in the variety of careers followed by its former pupils."

A list follows: in the period from 1841–1878, fifty-seven former pupils became teachers, eighteen missionaries, eight clerical workers, four nurses, three doctors, one school matron, one milliner, and thirty-seven became wives of ministers or missionaries. Those early school leavers were trailblazers of their day! However, a quick comparison with a selection of 1982 leavers (in the year when the school celebrated a century in its Sevenoaks home) shows how girls' choices had widened dramatically. These Sixth Formers were going off to study Civil Engineering, Architecture, Art, Medieval Studies, Medicine, Accountancy and Music, as well as the more traditional subjects.

Mrs Cheetham resigned in 1875, through ill health. She died in 1917. Her replacement, Miss Coleman, found the task of managing all

aspects of school life very onerous. In 1878 the formidable Miss Kate Unwin was appointed; she was to stay in her post for nearly twenty years.

Life in Walthamstow was changing as the century wore on. The coming of the railway in the 1870s had connected the pretty village to London itself. Building developments were mushrooming and the air (very much a preoccupation of the age) was becoming less pleasant. The prevailing winds, blowing from west to east, drove the fumes of the city towards Walthamstow. Moreover, as *The Christian World* reported, "Crowds of people come from London by train, and prevent the girls enjoying their walks as formerly." Estimates of population growth in London at this time suggest that, in the two decades between 1861 and 1881, the population grew by about a million people. No wonder the Marsh Street community were beginning to feel encroached upon!

With sixty pupils on the roll, and more asking to be admitted, the management concluded that "alterations and additions have been made till it is no longer possible to add or alter". It was time to move! But where should the new school be situated?

The search began. The Management Committee were looking for a site on which to build outside London, which was rapidly expanding into the suburbs, but not too far away from the school's birthplace. Mrs Foulger's daughter, now Mrs Pye-Smith, had married and moved to Sevenoaks and was living at St Katherine's, in the St. John's area of Sevenoaks. She wrote urging the claims of Sevenoaks, as a suitable place to build a new school. The "beautiful Kentish village" (*Christian World*, 1878) offered "loveliness of scenery and (a) reputation for health-giving properties". Just as importantly, if the school were to move to her home town, Mrs Pye-Smith could maintain links with her mother's school. In fact, Mrs Pye-Smith went on to support the school for forty-five years, and her daughters followed in her footsteps.

Sevenoaks, it was thus decided, would be the growing school's new home!

A suitable site was found in the Hollybush area, which was then largely given over to a few substantial houses, like Vine Court and Quakers Hall, with the remainder of the land used for farming. Sevenoaks School sold some of their land to the Walthamstow school (land which had been granted to them, as far back as the early 1500s, as playing fields.) The new school would enjoy open space all around it, although many houses sprang up in the St. John's area, towards the end of the century. In fact, there were more schools than one might imagine in this part of Sevenoaks, at the time of building the new Walthamstow Hall. (Some of them would have been very small establishments). St. John's National School,

1878: Laying the Foundation Stone of the new school in Sevenoaks: an invitation, a programme for the ceremony and a magazine report

the Cobden Road Schools, Sevenoaks Public Elementary School for Infants, Vine House School and Vine College were all neighbouring educational establishments of one kind or another, but, of course, their ethos and clientele were significantly different from the "Home and School".

On June 26th 1878, a special train from London brought about 150 well-wishers to Sevenoaks, for the laying of the Foundation Stone of Walthamstow Hall. The journey from Charing Cross took scarcely longer in those days than it does in 2013! The special train, conveying the guests to the ceremony, left Charing Cross at 11.55 am and arrived in Sevenoaks (at Bat and Ball station) forty-five minutes later, having called at Cannon Street en route.

Newspapers of the day report that a special tent was erected for the ceremony, which included a hymn, a prayer and an address. A special commemorative silver trowel was used to lay the Foundation Stone, the very same trowel that was used in 2013, at a ceremony to mark the start of the Junior School Dining Hall building project. However, as you may be able to see from the photograph, it does not look as if the trowel was used to spread cement!

In 1878, proceedings having been concluded, the special guests repaired to the Crown Hotel for lunch, just avoiding being caught in a severe thunderstorm. The Right Hon. W.E. Forster, a Liberal MP, had performed the ceremony of setting the first stone of the new school in its place. How fitting it was, that the author of the Elementary Education Act of 1870, which defined the format for the education of all children between the ages of five and twelve, in this country, should be the guest of honour. Walthamstow Hall, as the school would become known once it had moved to Sevenoaks, had been providing education for girls, from families of very modest means, for forty years!

It is tempting to wonder what Mr Forster's opinions might have been of the speech which was given at the celebration lunch on that day. The Reverend White was moved to announce that the girls of Walthamstow Hall would receive "just as good an education as their brothers". However, he went on to say that "men did not want companions who could do arithmetic better than they could, but women who were womanly". How odd that now sounds, to readers in the twenty-first century!

The Silver Trowel

The Montgomery Sisters and the Willow Sisters, all at school in the 1870s

Chapter 3: **1878-1898**

Life in the new school in Sevenoaks

The move to Hollybush Lane, Sevenoaks, would be hard work and it was fortunate that the Headmistress of the time, Miss Unwin, was very strong and capable. One of her members of staff recalled that she seemed to manage on five hours of sleep a night. She was the first Headmistress to be given, by the Management Committee, complete control of all the academic matters in the school. Like most Headmistresses of her time, she taught a full timetable, but also paused in the middle of a morning's teaching to help to prepare the lunch! She was one of a new generation of women who could experience exercising authority within her own domain. Had she

married she would, of course, have been forced to content herself with merely running her own household.

The fund-raising for the new school in Sevenoaks began. The Building Fund Accounts of the time tell us that sale of the property in Walthamstow raised £2,184. The new school building would be brand new, purpose built, designed by the architect Edward C. Robins, who also designed The North London Collegiate School for Girls and the Public Elementary Schools in Wapping. Many schools moved into a building that had been originally built for quite another purpose, perhaps as a large family

The builders outside the new school at Sevenoaks

An invitation, printed on silk, to the 1881 Fancy Fair

home. The girls and staff from Walthamstow could look forward to a building that had been specifically designed to meet the needs of a school of the time, and a boarding school at that.

Aspects of the new school's design would reflect the influence of the Arts and Crafts movement, whose founder, William Morris, had spent his early years in Walthamstow. The architect aimed to make the building look attractive, as well as ensuring it was functional. A glance up to the

exuberant sunflower patterns under the eaves shows that intention quite clearly. The estimated cost of the building project was £16,000, to be raised by subscription and fund-raising events. To judge the scale of the enterprise, it is interesting to learn that, in 1881 in Walthamstow, the cost of renting a family home was between 10 and 40 shillings per week (*The Suburban Homes of London, 1881*).

In 1881 a "Fancy Fair" was held at the Cannon Street Hotel in London over four days and succeeded in raising £2,700. The publicity for that event explains that the "Hall will be fitted up in the most attractive manner, as a Japanese village". The girls we are told performed the *Toy Symphony* and performed in dramatic tableaux.

The programme for a slightly later fund-raising event, in 1887, gives us an idea of the sort of things that were on sale at these "bazaars". In 1887 shoppers could buy Venetian glass, Russian jewellery, clothes for poor children and dolls' dress patterns, amongst many other delights. And at 3.00 pm Miss Headdon "demonstrated how to teach children household tasks using toys". We might wonder how many people queued up to watch!

Detail of the sunflowers in the eaves of the Arts and Crafts main building

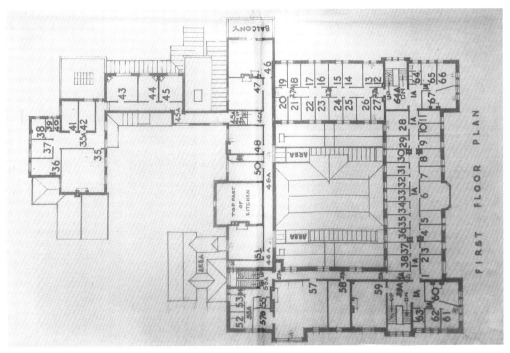

Architect's plan of the Arts and Crafts main building

The Arts and Crafts reception room as it appears in 2013

Boarders outside the main building of their new school

The new Sevenoaks building was finally opened on May 17th 1882. A newspaper account of the time gives it a very favourable report:

"The property consists of nearly four acres of land, so that, besides a garden large enough to give a good supply of fruit and vegetables, there is ample room for the children's enjoyment." There was accommodation for eighty-four girls, as well as the teaching and domestic staff.

The Walthamstow establishment had to move down to Sevenoaks in batches. Some of the staff arrived first to prepare for the girls. The interior was not quite complete, so that there were no railings on the stairs. Undaunted the teachers carried bedding up to the dormitories, in what is now the Erasmus building. The girls arrived on June 5th and settled in. They appreciated the fact

that each girl had her own little sleeping cubicle within the dormitories, so that she could call a small private space her own. As girls might not see their family homes for years, this was a thoughtful arrangement on the part of the school.

In the closing years of the nineteenth century, life at Walthamstow Hall, as the school would now be known, might seem very restricted by modern standards. Girls had little contact with the world outside school: they could not go out for tea, for fear of catching an infectious disease, there was no organised sport, only drill. Walks, in Knole Park and the Kent countryside, were taken in crocodile formation. Food was simple, Sundays were largely devoted to worship and Bible study and discipline was firm. However, there were lighter moments, when the girls could play outside, enjoy country dancing and play-acting and go on expeditions to Chevening, One Tree Hill and Fawke Common.

In a letter, which survives from 1889, a pupil, Ada Mary Cousins, gives news of school life. She had been tending her own garden plot:

"My garden is so pretty now, the girls are always admiring it. I have so many flowers out and it is so full, I have no room for seeds."

She goes on to bemoan the fact that she is only allowed one bath a week!

It does seem clear, from all the accounts that survive from this era, that the staff were dedicated to their work and watched over their pupils with great care, as well as setting them high standards of work and behaviour. Ella Hillier, a pupil in Miss Unwin's day, described her as "broadminded" and well she may have been for her times, but we might be surprised to learn that Miss Unwin was shocked to find young Ella reading *Jane Eyre,* which she proceeded to confiscate until the holidays!

Parents writing about the school in 1887 enthusiastically praised the way in which the institution was run. They referred to the "thoroughness of teaching" and the "robust health, cheerfulness of deportment and happiness of spirit" of the girls. One wrote that "Miss Unwin seems to take pleasure in making all her large adopted family happy". No doubt Miss Unwin did want to make the girls happy. But she could also seem very stern, with her insistence on the highest standards of Christian morality.

From the 1880s onwards, girls sat public examinations and began to aim high in the academic sphere. Alice Allen was the first girl to win a scholarship to Cardiff and Alice Hawker one of the first to undertake medical training, at the University of London. One of the treasures of the School Archive is the notebook that belonged to Alice's sister, Jessie, at school between 1882 and 1890. It resembles an autograph book; Jessie's friends have all inscribed favourite pieces of poetry, along with their signatures, and some have contributed accomplished watercolour illustrations.

A page from Jessie Hawker's notebook. The symbol of a ship has always had a special meaning for girls at Walthamstow Hall

Another much loved item in the Archive is a handwritten letter from "Minnie", dated 1882, giving her child's version of school news, to her parents:

"We have planted three chestnut trees in the middle of our playground and it will look very nice when it [sic] has its leaves on in the spring time.

We played up in the nursery instead of playing in the schoolroom and I liked it better.

There are only five more weeks till Christmas and I do not know where we are going at all."

This last comment reflects the fact that Minnie would have to be sent to some kind relatives or guardians for Christmas, as going home would be out of the question.

By the end of Miss Unwin's tenure in 1898, thirty-seven pupils sat public examinations, of whom eleven gained Honours. A rather sad footnote to these successes is a comment in Elsie Pike and Constance Curryer's "*The Story of Walthamstow Hall*": in 1887, a girl was awarded a scholarship to Girton College, Cambridge, but "since her parents thought the further pursuit of learning unwomanly, she entered the Post Office instead…"

A significant decision was taken in 1886: the school would admit pupils who were not daughters of missionaries, although many of them were the daughters of clergymen. Later still, in 1904, day girls would be admitted. These changes would gradually have a noticeable effect on the atmosphere of the school; interestingly, some of the early inspection reports comment favourably on the energising influence day girls brought to this somewhat cloistered community. One of the very last daughters of overseas missionaries to

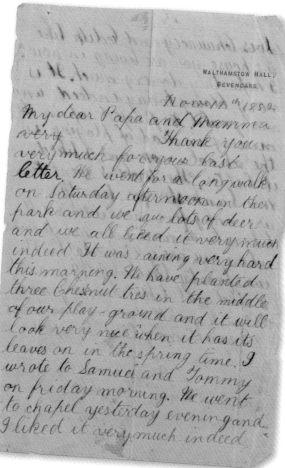

Letter from Minnie

attend Walthamstow Hall left in 2003. Writing in the *CODA* school magazine of that year, Jaime Moussa expressed feelings, which must have been shared by so many other girls, from generation to generation:

"I live astride two very different countries, two cultures. Imagine the countries as two floats. They must support me on the turbulent water we move across. I must balance."

Another important decision, made in 1897, was the purchasing of Knole Cottage, further down the lane from the main school, to become a sanatorium. Infectious diseases could be fatal in those days before modern medicines, and it was important, in a boarding school, to isolate the sufferers. Joyce Wilkins, who was a pupil in 1909, recalls how "if we were really ill, or the weather was bad, then we were taken down to the cottage in a large hooded Victorian bath-chair, which was drawn by Emery, the gardener's boy". The school of today still owns the bath-chair, although, fortunately, trips to the Medical Centre, involve no more than a short flight of stairs!

Grace Hutchinson was a pupil during the final years of Miss Unwin's reign. She has left us her memories of school life. We read of walks in Knole, where the girls would go looking for glow-worms in the dusk and of evening entertainments in the Dining Hall. Grace records her sadness that her friend Muriel Slater, who left school to become a nurse in South India, died of "the plague" within a year. The missionary life was still fraught with danger.

The "Black Maria", as it was called, which transported girls who were ill to the sanatorium

Chapter 4: 1898-1914

Difficult times on the horizon

After nineteen years of service Miss Unwin finally retired. It proved to be difficult to replace her and different arrangements were tried under Miss John, Miss Millar, Miss Condie and Miss Champness. This period also saw a worrying outbreak of diphtheria. To make matters worse, there were problems with the drainage, so serious that the girls had to be evacuated to St. Leonard's, while things were put right. What a relief it must have been when, in 1901, Miss Sophie Hare became the Headmistress of the school.

Miss Hare had new ideas for a new century. She reorganised the school day to allow more exercise and relaxation. She encouraged sport and the establishment of school clubs and societies and relaxed many of the rules, which had restricted the contact between the girls and people outside the school community. Oxford Extension lectures were begun at school in 1889. Best of all, perhaps, Miss Hare aimed to "give girls the maximum of intellectual freedom" (*The Story of Walthamstow Hall*). Her influence on her pupils was profound; "she was largely responsible for our future life-work," wrote one as she looked back on school life.

In her time, Miss Hare would have to deal with financial worries, epidemics and all the strain of running a boarding school during the First World War. Educated herself, at the North London Collegiate School, under the redoubtable Miss Buss, Miss Hare "showed care and interest... in each individual pupil under her charge". She had a "profound understanding of human nature". That did not mean that younger girls did not find her somewhat

Miss Hare and her pupils outside the front door in 1909

intimidating! Joyce Wilkins, aged six or seven, found her stern and awe-inspiring, but still managed to enjoy the nickname the girls gave her of "Soapy Hare". Joyce records, in her book *A Child's Eye View* (1992), how all the girls lined up each week, to say goodnight to Miss Hare, one by one, and to receive a kiss. That might seem odd to us, but Miss Hare, and all her staff, were only too aware of how the girls lacked the affection of parents.

Changes were afoot in the years before the war. In 1899, W.O.G.A (Walthamstow Old Girls' Association) had been launched, with Miss Pye-Smith, granddaughter of Mrs Foulger, as its first President. Their first newsletter was published in 1902; since that day the Association has gone from strength to strength. In 2013, its members now number more than

The Walthamstow Old Girls' Association handbook of 1901 listing its earliest members

1,000 and, just as in the early days, it is a source of friendship and support for all former pupils of the school.

Some years later, in 1918, a Junior W.O.G.A was formed, which gloried in the name of J.O.G.A.S (Junior Old Girls of Sevenoaks). The rule was that membership only lasted for five years after first leaving school; after that, former students were promoted to Walthamstow Old Girls' Association proper.

When, in 1903, the school was "recognised" as effective, by the local authority, it was the beginning of a new chapter in its life. The institution made the deliberate choice to make itself more publicly accountable. Thus, Miss Hare and the Governors arranged for the teaching of the school to be inspected by the University of London and for the girls to sit the university's examinations. Day girls were admitted from 1904, although one of the pioneers claimed she was regarded as a "freak" by the boarders. Soon, however, girls who were boarding were keen to be invited out to the homes of day girls.

Early inspection reports from 1906 onwards are mostly very complimentary, although there are strongly worded complaints about the lack of Science teaching (apart from Botany). The money was found and a Science classroom provided, so that, by 1912, the Inspectors were claiming that "the school may now challenge comparison with any girls' school, of a similar type". Two decades later, the Headmistress of the time, Miss Ramsay, was able to boast that Walthamstow Hall was the first girls' school in Kent to introduce Biology into the curriculum. Mrs Foulger and her friends, who founded the school, would also have rejoiced at a comment in the inspection report of 1919: "There is, happily, no 'institutional' feeling about it [the school]; it is more like a true home and the girls are contented and bright."

Proper Science facilities for girls: an early Science laboratory at Walthamstow Hall

Pupils in 2013 might not consider some aspects of early twentieth century school life all that homely! Helen Churcher, who attended the school in 1904, recalled Sunday dinners that made her shudder: cold meat, pickled beetroot and jacket potatoes, followed by stewed apples and custard. The restriction of hairwashing to twice a term would almost certainly horrify girls nowadays. But most painful of all, of course, was the separation from family. Helen felt very fortunate, as her parents, missionaries in Tunisia, could come to England once a year for summer holidays, whereas some of her friends endured long separations.

The school continued to flourish in the first years of the twentieth century: the 1901 Census records sixty-nine pupils in school. More accommodation was needed to cope with a changing curriculum. A Gymnasium was built, a Science room and a greenhouse added, the Cookery School was enlarged and a Hockey field purchased. Mr Buckland, the gardener, laid

out new fruit and vegetable gardens, growing much of the food used in the school kitchens. Mr Emery, who served as a gardener for fifty years, remembered the Hockey field in its early days. The grass was only mown once a year, with scythes, so that in the summer months the girls could completely hide from view, by lying down in the long grass!

The little girls boarding at the school, were catered for in their own Nursery and Night Nursery. *Wonderland* – a children's magazine of 1913 – reported to its young readers that the Day Nursery in the school contained "the biggest dolls' house we had ever seen, with all its rooms fully furnished". Archive photographs show this much loved plaything in pride of place.

Joyce Wilkins joined the school in 1909, at the age of six, and her memoirs give a detailed picture of school life before the First World War. She describes the furnishings of the Night Nursery: walls decorated with large pictures

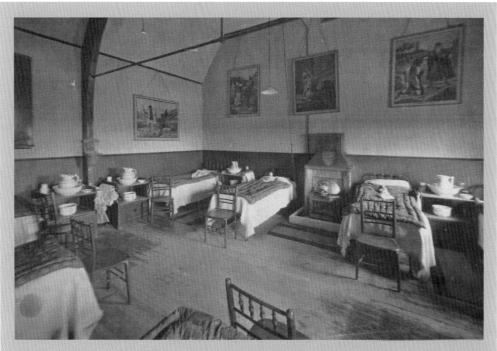

The Night Nursery, as Joyce Wilkins remembered it

Junior pupils enjoying music in the garden

*A dolls' house, once played with in the Nursery,
now conserved in the Archive*

of scenes from the Bible (her favourite was the *Lost Sheep*), a bed, chair and washstand for each little girl. Joyce, looking for a place of retreat, once climbed inside the drawer provided for her dirty clothes, managing to tip over the whole piece of furniture, breaking the china jug and bowl and spilling water everywhere. She felt humiliated. Joyce does not seem to have been punished on this occasion but certainly was soundly reprimanded for other crimes. Discipline was very strict by modern standards. No talking was allowed in the corridors or in the Dining Room, until a grace had been said. At meals no girl could help herself to any food, but must wait until her neighbour offered it. A Bible verse had to be learned – and repeated – every morning, and untidiness, lateness and poor work was severely castigated.

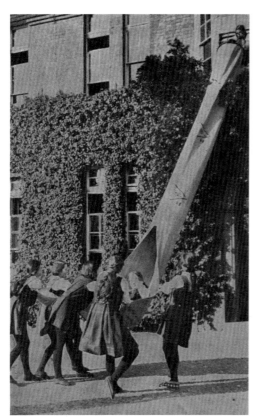

A dramatic moment in a school fire practice

The uniform of the time was rather severe in appearance too, with its navy calf-length skirt, white blouse and tie and black woollen stockings (and lines were issued to punish the breaking of uniform rules; allowing one's boater to slide off the back of the head was, for example, a punishable offence!). However, Prize Day offered some real excitement. On that occasion, the whole school demonstrated its efficient fire-drill routine to an admiring, and perhaps apprehensive, audience. All the girls climbed to the upper floors of the building. At a given signal, each one shot down to the ground in a linen tube, which acted as an emergency fire escape. Prefects took responsibility for sliding down first and steadying the mouth of the tunnel as each girl popped out, like a rabbit out of a hat. To round off the exciting display, the pupils marched on to the lawn and formed themselves into the shape of the letters WHSMD (Walthamstow Hall School for Missionary Daughters), accompanied, we imagine by enthusiastic applause!

Emmeline Blackburn (who went on to become Headmistress of the school) came to Sevenoaks, like Joyce, aged six years old. She and her sisters were day pupils. Her summer term report of 1917 survives in the Archive and tells us exactly what subjects little girls of that time were taught. Predictably, there is Reading, Writing and Arithmetic, but also History, Literature and Geography, taught through stories. In addition there is Nature Study, Drawing, Handwork, Singing and Drill. It seems quite a wide curriculum and certainly has many similarities with the subjects taught to children in the 1950s, with the possible exception of "Drill"!

In 1911 there were, according to the Census of that year, sixty-one pupils in residence, and eleven teaching staff. They were looked after by a team of sixteen domestic staff, four of whom were employed in the laundry. The school had its own special laundry building, to deal with all the washing created by a community of schoolgirls. Two Nurses, a Housekeeper and two Matrons, along with a variety of gardeners and groundsmen, completed the picture.

Girls on Prize Day seated on the front lawn, forming the letters WH

Emmeline Blackburn in 1917

This period was marked by a drama enacted "behind the scenes", which caused Miss Hare to tender her resignation, in May 1913. The problem centred on the fact that Miss Hare had serious objections to some of the opinions of the local Congregational Church Minister and declined to attend services. She also allowed the girls to opt out of Sunday worship. This was very embarrassing for the Management Committee, as much of the school's funding came from church congregations like this one. Miss Hare was adamant. On no account would she change her views. Thus, an advertisement was placed in the paper for a new Principal, (a member of a free church and "preferably" a graduate – note the order of priorities). However, the Committee was by no means unanimous that Miss Hare must go. Some felt she was extravagant – electric lighting was installed in the school in 1913, at the shocking cost of £200! Yet she clearly was a very capable

Girls in a lesson. Notice that girls were seated individually - no pair work or group work here!

woman: the Board of Education Report of 1915 found that she "kept in touch with every part of the school" and that her handling of finance was skilful and economical". Somehow a truce was reached, Miss Hare remained, and stayed at the helm throughout the war years.

With hindsight, it is easy to imagine that people living in the early twentieth century felt the shadow of war approaching. However, school life seems to have gone on much as usual, although financial difficulties were becoming more apparent. Perhaps surprisingly, Easter 1914 saw the first school trip to France: a group of nineteen boys and girls, drawn from Eltham College and Walthamstow Hall, set off to walk from Boulogne to Calais. How tragic that, all too soon, some of those Eltham boys would revisit those places along the French coast, never to come home again.

Chapter 5: 1914-1938

War and a one hundredth birthday

It was not long before the shadows of war reached the school in Sevenoaks. Local troops dug practice trenches in Knole Park (and the girls played inside them!); the sounds could be heard of soldiers drilling in Hollybush Lane. The school declined to allow the soldiers to drill in the school Gymnasium, when it was requested. Some foods were in short supply, especially meat, butter, sugar and cheese. In 1914, the minutes of a House Committee meeting record that "Emery required manure for vegetables" and that the "profit on pigs for six months was £5 -12s -7d". Fortunately for the school, Emery was busy trying to provide as much food as possible from the school grounds. Even so, we learn that the cook was moved to make jam from carrot and tomato, or date and rhubarb, as sugar could not be bought. Joyce Wilkins and friends kept bees to provide some sweetness in the form of honey.

> The First World War
>
> When the First World War was on
> The girls gathered round and had a song
> While bombs and shrapnels fast fell down
> They sang by candles in their dressing gowns.

At Prize Day in 1915, the girls decided to forgo prizes, instead donating the money to war funds – to Polish and Serbian Relief charities and the Sevenoaks V.A.D. nursing fund. The consequences of war would have quickly become apparent to those associated with the school. By December 1915, eight young men of the Pye-Smith family (Mrs Foulger's descendants) were on active service and seventy former Eltham College boys had joined up. Soon the grim recording of deaths began. Walthamstow Old Girls'

Girls hard at work in their school garden

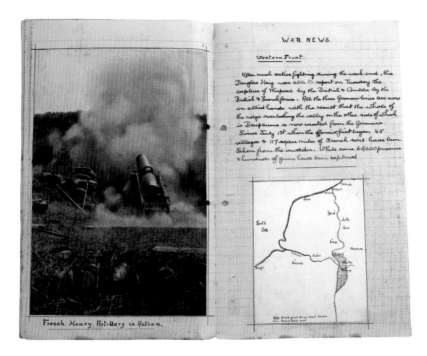

One of several scrapbooks kept by pupils, charting the progress of the war

Association newsletters of the period gave the sad news of the loss of many brothers, cousins, fiancés and friends:

"On May 15th 1917, killed in action by a shell in France, Lieut. PHG Pye-Smith of the Liverpool Regiment, aged 21."

"On July 3rd, in France, leading his platoon, though shot in the thigh, Siegfried Thomas Hinkley, son of the Rev. W. and Mrs Hinkley of Anantapur, South India, aged 19."

There were dangers at school too. The girls in Sevenoaks experienced air raid warnings, but there were no shelters to run to. Instead, everyone gathered in the school Dining Hall and sang or danced to take their minds off possible dangers. The young Emmeline Blackburn remembered "the searchlights criss-crossing the sky, as we walked past The Vine cricket ground in the darkness".

Like many people, the girls feared an invasion by enemy troops. They were instructed to keep a small suitcase ready-packed in their cubicles; the staff also had cases at the ready, as well as £2 in silver, and the list of the seven or eight girls they would each take with them, if the order came to flee.

The privations of war continued. It was horribly cold in 1917 and fuel was extremely scarce. Strict blackout precautions were in place and all travel severely restricted. Missionary parents faced serious dangers if they attempted to travel to England to see their children – and many could not make the journey. Mail was delayed, rationing became stricter, even stationery was so expensive, that girls used old envelopes for rough working. And then came the influenza epidemic of 1918. Large numbers were extremely ill; the school closed completely from mid-November to January 7th. Sadly, a pupil and teacher at Walthamstow Hall died of the disease, so that the Armistice Day, marking the end of the war, was overshadowed with sadness. The six girls at school still free from illness marked the occasion by attending a thanksgiving service, and by eating as much bread and jam for tea as could be found, while all the lights streamed out through the uncurtained windows.

One might have thought that the ending of war would bring easier times for the school. The truth was that the financial situation had been growing ever worse. In 1919 there were sixty-three boarders, forty-three day girls and ten "lay boarders" (girls whose fathers were not clergymen.) Their fees just did not cover the costs of running the school. Eltham College was in the same difficulties. The Annual Meeting Report of 1920 adopted a grave tone: "Both schools are in a very critical financial position and Walthamstow Hall has to face a debt of £762."

The decline in the numbers of married men taking up missionary work overseas meant that there were fewer "missionary sons and daughters" needing the particular type of provision offered by the two schools. For example, in 1919, 185 men were posted abroad by the London Missionary Society and ninety women. Twenty years later only 152 men were serving as missionaries, while of the 118 women serving overseas, most were unmarried. That meant that the schools could not count on such a steady supply of pupils as in former years.

Desperate times call for serious measures. In 1921, the schools negotiated an agreement with Kent Education Committee, which would make a considerable change to the way in which pupils were recruited. Having begun as a private boarding school for the daughters of missionaries, Walthamstow Hall would now have to guarantee to offer a percentage of free places to pupils from local elementary schools. In return, it would receive an annual grant to boost its funds.

Eltham College and Walthamstow Hall joined forces to launch an appeal for funds to "Save the Schools", setting a target of £10,000. Much was made of the symbol of a ship in the fund-raising literature; it served as a poignant reminder of how the children in the care of the two institutions had waved their parents off on long sea voyages, to mission stations, thousands of miles away. They had sailed *"from Sevenoaks to the Seven Seas"*. The design of the little booklet, which launched the Ship Theatre redevelopment Appeal in 2013, draws its inspiration directly from the design of the fund-raising literature of the 1920s.

Appeal booklets, past and present, both employ the image of a ship on its voyage

Two views of school life from staff photo albums of the period: a classroom for the youngest pupils and the Dining Hall

"I always feel that, whether I am at Sevenoaks or at Pontesford, I am at Walthamstow Hall", she wrote.

Back in Sevenoaks things were not getting easier. It became very difficult to recruit domestic staff; help in the school kitchen was down to a minimum, so much so, that day girls had to eat lunch at the British Restaurant, in Sevenoaks. On walks in Knole Park girls followed Government advice to collect nettles, for use in their dinners. One former pupil did not enjoy this delicacy: "They would have been tasty, if only the kitchen staff had cooked them sufficiently to prevent us being stung". At Pontesford, rose hips were gathered on country walks – 40lbs at a time – to be made into rose hip syrup for babies.

Lessons and, more seriously, public examinations were interrupted by air raids. Sometimes the girls were told to duck beneath their desks, if the alarm might pass quickly. Otherwise all must troop down into the trenches and finish the exam paper underground! It happened so often that it became almost routine. Ann Reynolds wrote to Catherine in 1944, "We are sick of going to the trenches so much." But she gives a clue, later in her letter, of what a frightening experience a raid could be. A landmine had just fallen and Ann recalled the moment:

"A wind went through the trenches and my eyes felt all funny – they still do three days afterwards."

There were, by contrast, a surprising number of brighter moments: *The Rose and the Ring* was performed by a cast of girls from school and boys evacuated from Shooters Hill in London (although it seems to have been a struggle to get the boys to rehearsals); other concerts and plays followed, including Gilbert and Sullivan's *HMS Pinafore*. There were school dances, for which girls prepared hand-painted dance programmes, so that dancers could book a partner for the Foxtrot or the Dashing White Sergeant in advance.

All through the war years and beyond, the energetic and enterprising Young Farmers' Club (YFC) members were busy rearing their pigs, poultry, rabbits, heifers and goats. In 1945 there were about one hundred members! The club's meticulous records still survive so that we know, for example, that Gillian Northfield was the "Leader of the Pullets poultry group" but also had a Young Farmers' plot to tend and helped with the harvest on a local farm. Rosemary Baker was in charge of a guinea pig family, went on visits to the blacksmith's and worked in local orchards, picking apples and plums. The photographs of YFC activities show competent, lively girls with impressive skills; being a club member involved rather more than simply stroking rabbits!

In 1942, Miss Ramsay wrote: "We must prepare our children to be social adventurers… The spirit of adventure is in our heritage – delight in simple things is our tradition." This combination of enjoying new challenges, while being content with a fairly simple style of life, seems to have helped the Walthamstow Hall community weather the War years.

The raids were still frequent, in the summer of 1944, so that on Prize Day, "The prizes were given on the front lawn and the meeting was punctuated with interludes down the trenches." However, by December it was considered safe to bring the Juniors back from Pontesford House to take up residence in Spicer House, which would provide a homely setting for them. Six new girls joined the school in 1945, having been held in Japanese war camps; they must surely have much needed a place to call "home".

Who knows how things might have developed in the post-war years, had it not been for the Butler Education Act of 1944? Under the provisions of the Act, the school became a Direct Grant School and was required to give free places to at least 25% of its pupils. Arrangements were also put in place to make funds available to assist missionary parents to pay the fees. In addition, the Trust Fund, built up by charitable donations, and administered by the school, could also provide help to families of limited means. This Butler Act had a decisive effect on the school's fortunes at this point: its finances were put on a reasonably secure footing, fees did not have to be increased, which might put them beyond the reach of some parents, and the school retained independence. The numbers on roll show a school flourishing: in the autumn of 1947, pupils numbered 334, of whom a hundred were boarders.

After twenty-four years of captaining the ship, it was time for Miss Ramsay to step down. She must have been delighted that she was able to appoint one of her own former pupils, Emmeline Blackburn, to succeed her as Headmistress (and Miss Blackburn, in her time, taught five future Headmistresses, including Mrs Lang, who became Headmistress of Walthamstow Hall, in 1984). Writing of Miss Ramsay, Miss Blackburn said, "She was the soul of generosity: her time, her possessions, her great warm personality were all given in overflowing measure to her work for this school." A typical mark of this generosity was Miss Ramsay's plan to set up a fund, as a retirement present, which would allow the school to enjoy many "Ramsay Occasions" in the future. These were intended to be interesting events – talks, films, demonstrations – which would venture into areas outside the curriculum. Thus, in 1987, for example, forty

A Physical Education lesson in the Junior School Hall

Girls enjoying their leisure time in a Common Room

years on from her retirement, the girls could watch a demonstration of holograms as a "Ramsay Occasion". And there have been many other similar occasions since.

Retirement celebrations were held for Miss Ramsay, presentations and speeches given. The work of post-war reconstruction had begun once more, just as it had done in 1914. Links with schools in Europe were quickly re-established and plans made to restructure the curriculum. A particularly interesting development would be a new General Course for the Sixth Form, imaginatively wide in its ambitions, which included an unusual course in Applied Design for non-specialists.

Ellen Catling, looking back on her days as a pupil in Miss Ramsay's time, reminds us that all of us will have uniquely personal memories of our connections with Walthamstow Hall, which form no part of an "official school history":

"I think perhaps we remember the important things. For me they are the sight of dragonflies over the pond, English and Greek plays of Euripides... licking my wooden spoon after

cake-making in the Cookery School... and poems read by Miss Ramsay."

At Speech Day in 1946, Miss Ramsay looked back at the school's past 108 years and then she looked forward to the future. This is what she said:

"This school has a unique heritage... Our founders, who planted the acorn one hundred and eight years ago in Walthamstow must surely rejoice when they see our Sevenoaks oak, which has survived the storm and blast and is spreading its branches ever wider, and which they planted in the faith – a faith on which we build that 'Except the Lord build the house, they labour in vain that build it.'"

Time has moved on, the oak has continued to spread its branches, for 175 years! Think back to five small girls, learning their letters in a schoolroom, in a pretty village close to London, as Victoria ascended the throne. Then marvel at how Mrs Foulger's first idea for a home and school, for the daughters of missionaries, grew and grew, and bore fruit!

(The story continues as an illustrated timeline.)

Headmistresses

Miss Blackburn 1946-1970

Miss Ramsay 1922-1946

Miss Unwin 1878-1898

Mrs Lang 1984-2002

Miss Hare 1901-1922

Miss Davies 1970-1983

Mrs Milner 2002-present day

Mrs Cheetham 1859-1875

Timeline
1945-1955

*Netball Team
1946-1947*

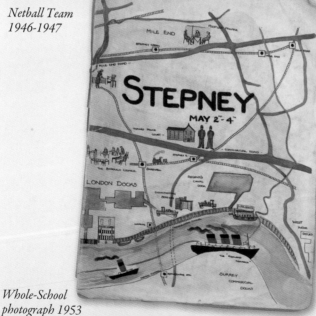

*Whole-School
photograph 1953*

1946 Miss Ramsay retired, Miss Blackburn took over. Christmas greetings broadcast abroad by boarders.

1947 First printed copy of school magazine since the war. Food parcels collected for the Save Europe Now charity.

1948 Margaret Bondfield, first woman Cabinet Minister is guest of honour at Speech Day.

School welcomes 12 German women visitors on an educational visit.

1949 School film is made. General Inspection (first for 20 years).

Sixth Form residential visit to Stepney to study social conditions.

1950 BBC Christmas broadcast for parents in Africa and India.

Opening of new Assembly Hall in Knole View (Juniors moved here in 1939).

1951 *GCE Ordinary and Advanced Level exams replaced School Certificate and Higher Certificate.*

Mr Emery, the gardener, completed 50 years' service.

1952 Junior Discussion Club (of 78 members) features Astronomy, Egyptian Archaeology and Stagecraft in their programme.

1953 *Coronation of Queen Elizabeth II.*

New Assembly Hall and other buildings replaced those damaged by war. *Merchant of Venice* performed in new hall. Quebec and Chartwell formed to create 6 houses.

Old Girls' Weekend in school to tour new accommodation.

1954 *The Treasury of the Kingdom*, a widely used anthology of religious writing, compiled by Miss Blackburn and colleagues, was published.

First inter-house Drama competition.

School fund-raising for new women's college at Cambridge.

1955 Production of *St. Joan*.

School Council votes to fine girls for leaving their property unmarked!

Talk from a member of the team that conquered Everest.

St. Joan

The front of the school from a time when there was no need for a car park

WALTHAMSTOW HALL
MAGAZINE

NON PALMA
SINE PULVERE

The Playroom for the Juniors

Timeline
1956-1965

An Art class at work

Junior School Christmas Play

1956 School Council debated Prefects wearing gowns and rejected the compulsory wearing of panama hats in the summer term.

1957 School held an Elizabethan Fair.

1958 Production of *A Midsummer Night's Dream*.

1959 World Refugee Year; school play *Noah* raised money for this cause.

1960 General Inspection of School. Building Fund for new Science Block established.

1961 Girls told they would lose house points for eating lollies in school uniform!

1962 The Bishop of Rochester, the Right Rev. R.D. Say, guest of honour at Speech Day.

Boarders enjoying some quiet time

Working with clay

Educated at
Walthamstow Hall

On the third floor at Peter Jones, in the Schoolwear
Department, parents and girls will find the clothes
that the school requires. From the large stock
of regulation schoolwear choice of an outfit at the
right price to suit a girl of any size is much simpler
than it has ever been. And parents who shop for
quality and hard wear will be in complete agreement
with daughters who, having looked to Peter Jones for their
schoolwear, will know where to shop in the
years to come for the clothes that matter.

dressed by

Peter Jones
SLOANE SQUARE LONDON SW1

A BRANCH OF THE JOHN LEWIS PARTNERSHIP

1963 125th anniversary of school's foundation.

Opening of new Science Block.

First male full-time member of teaching staff joined the school.

1964 Land purchased to provide room for 3 additional courts and a pool.

Voluntary Service Unit established jointly with Sevenoaks School.

Hugh Goffe Foundation set up: it would help to fund a number of overseas students.

1965 School voted for *Winnie the Pooh* as its favourite book; *Gone with the Wind* came second.

Learning needlework skills

Prefects with Miss Blackburn

Timeline
1966-1975

KENT COUNTY FEDERATION Y.F.C's

21ST BIRTHDAY PARTY
at
WALTHAMSTOW HALL, SEVENOAKS

on Saturday 22nd January 1966.
PROGRAMME:—

2.P.M. mounts— COUNTRY FOLK DANCING & singing
led by Mr Brian Heritcan— S.E. Area Organiser of
"English Folk Dance & Song Society"

2·30 Pm. Official welcome to all visitors
During the afternoon, short entertainments will be given by
The JUDD, NORTHFLEET, OLDBOROUGH MANOR, RAMSDEN, K.
SEVENOAKS SCHOOL Y.F.C'S
Time for viewing DISPLAYS exhibits

4 P.M. LIGHT REFRESHMENTS—
                        a) Early Federation Days—
4·45 pm. Final Entertainment.— b) South of British Rabbit Council
R.S.V.P. giving approximate numbers.   5.20 pm bus dispose
donations. Accurate expenses. There will be a plate for small
                                    donations. any surplus donated will be sent to K.P.Y.F.C's

Spicer House playroom drawn by a pupil

1966 Opening of Swimming Bath.

21st Anniversary of the Young Farmers' Club.

1967 Dedication of the Carol Hasler Room, (now the Quiet Room).

1968 1st Lacrosse Team won All England Tournament.

School Voluntary Service Unit is filmed.

1969 *First man on the moon.*

Sixth Form Society launches Mechanics group (in addition to Shooting, Judo, Badminton, Table Tennis, etc.).

1970 Miss Blackburn retired; Miss Davies appointed as Headmistress.

"Brentnor" opened as Sixth Form Centre.

The Tennis Team of 1970

1971 Numbers of VSU
volunteers reach 100.

Production of
Oedipus Rex.

1972 Judo club set up.

Summer Enrichment
Day of talks given
on Prisons, Nursing,
Computers and
Good Grooming.

1973 *The Story of
Walthamstow Hall*,
originally published
in 1938, revised,
reprinted and
extended.

1974 Salmon Wing opened.

3-day Sixth Form
Reading Party in
Blackburn House.

1975 School became
completely
independent as Direct
Grant phased out.

Bursary provision
established and
extended from
this year.

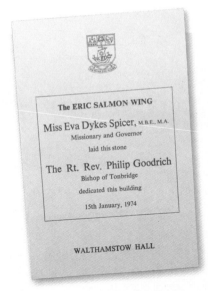

The ERIC SALMON WING

Miss Eva Dykes Spicer, M.B.E., M.A.
Missionary and Governor

laid this stone

The Rt. Rev. Philip Goodrich
Bishop of Tonbridge

dedicated this building

15th January, 1974

WALTHAMSTOW HALL

*The Dining Room - perhaps one of the least
changed rooms in the school*

Prefects with Miss Davies

The Carol Hasler Room in use

Timeline

1976-1985

1976 Easter Bonnet competition

1952 1977

JUBILEE CONCERT

1976 "Friends of Walthamstow Hall" organisation launched.

Direct Grant status of school abolished.

1977 Jubilee Concert to celebrate the Queen's Silver Jubilee.

1978 German and French exchanges to Ober-Ramstadt and Pontoise began.

1979 *First British woman Prime Minister.*

Computer Studies became part of the curriculum.

1980 "Friends of Walthamstow Hall" changed its name to "Friends and Parents".

1981 Walthamstow Hall joined 220 schools in offering Assisted Places.

Boarders' Common Room

Bedtime in a Junior boarding house

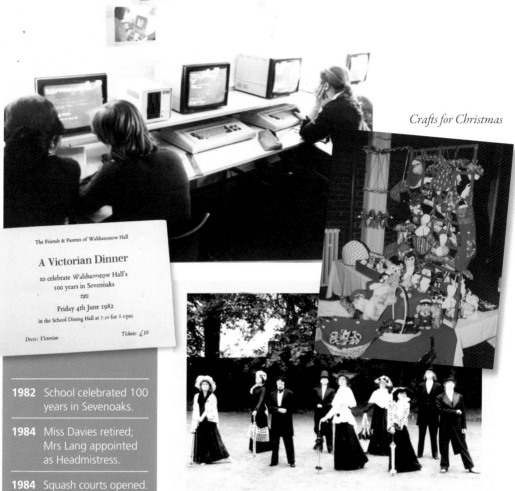

Crafts for Christmas

The Friends & Parents of Walthamstow Hall

A Victorian Dinner

to celebrate Walthamstow Hall's
100 years in Sevenoaks
꧁꧂
Friday 4th June 1982
in the School Dining Hall at 7.30 for 8.0pm

Dress: *Victorian*   Tickets: £10

1982 School celebrated 100 years in Sevenoaks.

1984 Miss Davies retired; Mrs Lang appointed as Headmistress.

1984 Squash courts opened.

Houses divided into house tutorial groups.

Work experience instituted.

Sir Jeremy Elwes (after whom the Elwes Drama Studio is named) is Chair of Governors.

1985 Senior boarders moved into Unwin House.

Production of *My Fair Lady*.

Some of the cast of My Fair Lady

Taken, developed and printed by
Giovanna Crozzi

The school in 1983 photographed by a pupil

Timeline

1986-1995

The Apple Tree Cottage reunion

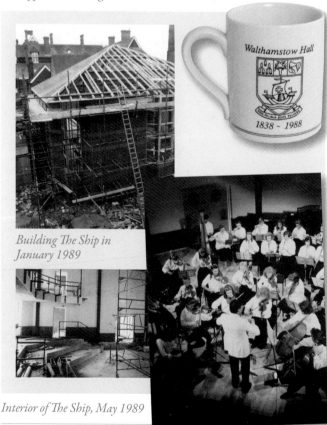

Building The Ship in January 1989

Interior of The Ship, May 1989

1986 Junior Choir participated in the Nice Festival.

Apple Tree Cottage reunion held for members of the original Form Two A.

1987 *The Great Storm (often called "The Hurricane") hit Britain in October.*

Worst snowfall in 40 years isolates Sevenoaks and surrounding villages.

1988 School's 150th anniversary celebrated with a service in Westminster Chapel, ball, concert, fun day, and exhibition of the school's history, sponsored by Liberty.

Gift of mulberry tree from the Junior School planted.

GCSE exams began.

1989 Opening of The Ship Theatre by renowned baritone Sir Geraint Evans.

Sir Geraint Evans

2 additions to the school's history published: *The Ship's Log* and Audrey Third and Anne Evans's continuation of *The Story of Walthamstow Hall.*

1990 Third Form visit Bruges for the Combined Arts Project.

1991 First Ship Festival.

1992 Merger of St. Hilary's School with Walthamstow Hall. Plan for Juniors to move to St. Hilary's site. School Council votes for new red uniform.

1993 Seeds from tree planted at David Livingstone's grave (sent to school as a memento of his family links with Walthamstow Hall) sown by school gardener – and they grew!

1994 A former pupil becomes one of the first women to be ordained Priest in the Church of England.

Sale of Ramsay and Spicer Houses to become family homes.

1995 Joint trip to Germany with Tonbridge School.

School celebrates anniversary of VE Day.

First Lacrosse Tour to USA.

School wins Science School of the Year Award.

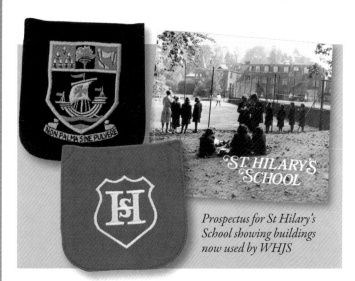

Prospectus for St Hilary's School showing buildings now used by WHJS

The Ship Festival of 1991 - Mrs Lang and special guest cut the cake

Growing the seeds from the tree at Livingstone's Grave

Timeline

1996-2005

The new library built above the Salmon Wing

Junior School girls in the new 'red' school uniform

1996 Emmeline Blackburn House opened as Sixth Form centre.

1997 New Library opened by the author, Susan Hill. Her most famous book is *The Woman in Black*.

Mrs Lang President of the G.S.A.

Assisted Places removed from school by local authority.

1998 Community play *The Oak, the Vine and the Mulberry Tree* devised in conjunction with local schools and residents.

Launch of Millennium Bursary Scheme to help some families with fees.

1999 Walthamstow Hall Old Girls' Association celebrated its 100th birthday.

Lacrosse Teams twice County Champions: First Team and Under-15s.

2000 *AS and A2 examinations introduced.*

UVI English students make pilgrimage to Bronte country.

The set design for The Oak, the Vine and the Mulberry Tree

2001 ISI School Inspection.

School Ski Team set up.

Friends and Parents Silver Jubilee; gift to Junior School of The Ark playground shelter.

The boarders' last Christmas.

2002 Walthamstow Hall becomes a girls' day school.

Mrs Milner appointed as Headmistress.

Latin added to the curriculum for all Third Form.

2003 Mr Ian Philip elected as Chair of Governors.

Erasmus Centre opened.

Spanish added to the curriculum.

2004 New Junior School Science laboratory opened.

Juniors become IAPS swimming record-holders.

2005 Trips to Berlin and Barcelona.

"Ramsay Occasion": Film Editor of *Harry Potter* films spoke to school.

Production of *South Pacific*.

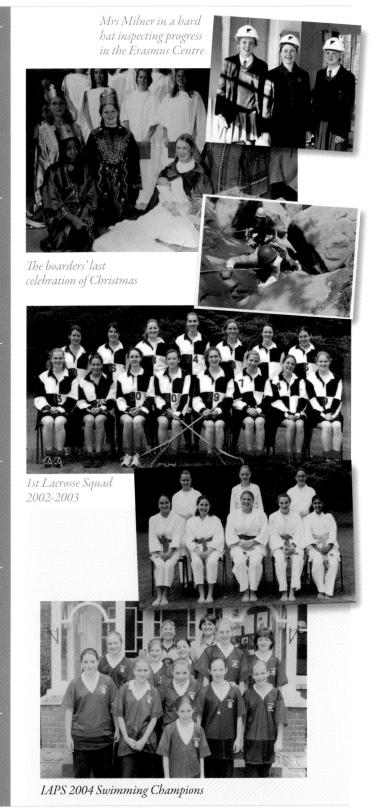

Mrs Milner in a hard hat inspecting progress in the Erasmus Centre

The boarders' last celebration of Christmas

1st Lacrosse Squad 2002-2003

IAPS 2004 Swimming Champions

Timeline

2006-2013

The new swimming pool, opened in 2008

The school production of Nicholas Nickleby, 2011

2006 Creation of new pond and wildlife areas.

LV trip to Oxford.

2007 ISI inspection describes the school as Outstanding.

The Ship Festival featured *The Sixteen* and also Wendy Cope.

2008 New Swimming Pool and Mulberry Sports Hall opened.

School Archives began the move to their new home.

2009 Maths Suite and Elwes Drama Studio opened.

First carol service for school and parents held at Tonbridge Chapel.

Production of *Fiddler on the Roof*.

2010 First Pre-U examinations sat.

Downton Music Room created.

Old Laundry converted into Design and Technology Studio. New subject of D&T on the curriculum.

2011 First "Strictly Wally" competition held.

First "Wally Pop" concert for charity.

The school production of She Stoops to Conquer

*175th Anniversary Service of
Thanksgiving at St Nicholas Church*

2012 *The Olympic Games
took place in London.*

Walthamstow Hall
celebrates
the Olympics.

Opening of The Hub.

2013 175th Anniversary
celebrations: May
Ball, Thanksgiving
Service, Junior School
tea party, launch of
Anniversary Appeal to
refurbish The Ship.

June 26th:
Ceremony to mark
the commencement
of the building of the
new Junior School
Dining Hall exactly
135 years after the
Foundation Stone
was laid at the Senior
School site. The
commemorative
silver trowel first
used in 1878 is used
once more!

2014 Publication of new
version of the written
school history.

Lower IV trip to the Paralympics, 2012

The Junior School celebrates the 175th Anniversary, 2013

Voices from 2013 - The Head Girls

"2013 has been a special year for me at Wally as it was my last year at school. The Upper Sixth are lucky to lead many of the most exciting events of the year including the Christmas panto and house events. We performed a version of *Shrek*, which took place in Far Far Away and saw Fiona (the Wally girl) and Shrek living happily ever after in the Wally Hall Castle. Although Upper Sixth is very stressful due to UCAS applications and A levels, combined with all these extra responsibilities that we take on, it is equally rewarding. The friendships that we have built over the last seven years are forged more strongly than ever and the relationships with teachers become full of respect."

Rosemary Barker, Head Girl 2012–2013, Medicine at St. Catherine's College, Oxford

"My proudest moments at Wally Hall have to include being elected Deputy Head Girl and winning the Young Enterprise County Speaking competition. The experience built my confidence and gave me an opportunity to speak to an audience about a topic I was so passionate about. I could not have succeeded without the unfailing support of my fellow team members, friends and Wally Hall staff. It was an amazing experience, which will stay with me forever."

Lucy Reid, Deputy Head Girl 2012–2013, Broadcast Journalism, Leeds

"I remember my first day of Sixth Form being just as great as my first day of Year 7, even with an induction day to ease us into the new roles we were to play within the school. To me Sixth Form meant a new identity, a fresh start and new possibilities. It suddenly dawned on me how the year group was beginning to mould itself into a new and diverse body, as the independence to choose our own subjects and follow our own interests developed our personalities and interactions with other students. Of course, the transition was never entirely easy, with learning to use self-discipline in "frees" and succumb to the explicit working conditions of the "Quiet Room" being two of our many "learning curves!""

Emily Bullman, Deputy Head Girl 2012–2013, Modern and Medieval Languages at Corpus Christi, Cambridge

"A typical 2013 Wally day begins with our form discussing everything from homework to weekend plans. On Mondays, Wednesdays and Fridays the whole school joins for Prayers in the Hall, where prefects stand in the aisles ensuring that all the students are quiet; this is called "ssh-ing", a very original name! Depending on the day either I or the Deputy Head Girls, will "beadle" and collect Mrs Milner to go to prayers. In Sixth Form we spend our lunchtime in our Common Room in EBH, with the occasional trips down to Rafferty's for hot chocolate! The Common Room is never full as we are involved in so many extra-curricular activities; Lacrosse and Netball practices, Choir and Drama rehearsals, which were very frequent this year due to the 175th gala performances of the musical *Guys and Dolls*."

Elizabeth Fitzpatrick, Head Girl 2013–2014

"A day as a Wally girl in 2013 begins with Sixth Form gathering in their territory, EBH (Emmeline Blackburn House), with two Common Rooms for the two separate years: an almost excessively spacious one for UVI, and a slightly cosier LVI one, as well as classrooms, including the History room, guarded by the ever-watchful eye of Barack Obama's life-size cardboard cut-out. The rest of the school rarely strays down there. Prayers is perhaps one of the most unique features of Wally as I know it; the entire school community gathers in the school Hall three times a week, with the Prefects on "ssh-ing duty", patrolling the edges of the room and taming the younger years. Currently, the school day is split into eight periods, but for the most part, from Year 10 and above, most lessons consume a double period. Up to UV, classes consist of up to twenty girls, while in Sixth Form, class sizes are smaller, allowing fierce debate, rapid learning and the development of a close relationship with peers and teachers alike.

Although Wally has undergone a number of changes since I joined the school six years ago – including the building of the swimming pool, the Downton Music Room, Elwes Drama Studio, Design Technology Studio and the Hub to name just a few – the same traditions remain, and underpin the daily routine of every Wally girl. The most considerable change experienced by Sixth Formers is perhaps the concept of us all growing up, maturing, shaped by the school community that surrounds us on a daily basis. I am sure that elements of Wally will still be recognisable in us all, as well as in future pupils, long after our Wally days are over.

Joanna Kaye, Deputy Head Girl 2013–2014

"As I enter the Upper Sixth, my past six years at Wally seem to have raced by, yet at the same time I feel so at home that I forget I was ever anywhere else. During my time here, I've seen how people aren't afraid to give everything a go, and often excel. Not being a huge school gives Wally a great advantage, with everyone able to make the most of the facilities and opportunities. I think this is essential to the tight community atmosphere found here, as the friendships between year groups and good relationships between students and staff would not exist otherwise. I believe our ethos and community from the very beginning of the school are what allow Wally to be such a happy place, and enable us as students to flourish more and more every year."

Emma Smith, Deputy Head Girl 2013–2014

Voices from 2013 - The 2013 Leavers

"Some of my favourite Wally moments have been those just prior to big events, most memorably before the "secret" pantomime, and in the last hour before the House Music Competitions. These times are always alive with activity – at Christmas with the whispered rumours of what the Upper Sixth have chosen for their pantomime, followed by the mad rush to the Hall, all under the pretence of a carol practice. The hyperactive mood experienced all at once by the school, the Christmas-cracker hats still balancing on our heads from the best lunch of the year, Christmas songs on our lips...

Before House Music, House Captains are wildly handing out house-coloured face paint, declaring war on their rival houses. Girls are rushing to last-minute rehearsals, frantically pulling on absurd costumes. The general atmosphere of friendly competition is one I'll certainly miss, but perhaps even more than that, the sense of pure "Wally spirit". The willingness to smear our faces with eye shadow and take the risk of swaying on the wobbly stands, all for the sheer fun of the afternoon. For the joy we always manage to find, singing songs we'd never heard of before, maybe off-key, maybe out of time with the piano, but together.

I also vividly remember one summer term, when House Athletics had to be cancelled due to a sudden downpour of rain. It was decided that it was too late to run lessons, so we all piled into The Ship, which was empty of chairs, along with our melting ice lollies, and sat on the floor and watched a classic film. This, for me at least, captured some of the true spirit of Wallies – the spontaneity, sense of fun and sense of family – the whole school spending an afternoon in The Ship Theatre, refusing to be perturbed by the downpour, oblivious to the horrible weather."

Rachael Newton, Classical Studies and Philosophy at Exeter

"What I love most about Wally is how accepting it is. I've had all my best memories here. Now that I am close to leaving I remember all the fun times I have had: climbing through the Salmon Wing window and getting caught by Miss Burtenshaw, valiantly trying out for the Lacrosse Team when I have the coordination of a fish, staying in the Dining Hall for the whole of lunch break just to carry on eating, getting unbelievably stressed as House Captain in the week of House Music, getting lost on the way to Young Enterprise, when I was in charge of the map!"

Ayesha Hussain,
Mathematics at Durham

"Looking back at my time at Wally, one of the memories that particularly comes back is the House Music Competitions. I am not at all musical so hours of trying to sing in tune ought not to have happy associations. However, something has changed now that my last House Music is behind me. Even while the rehearsals were the bane of my spring term and I know that I hated the time I spent in hot Erasmus classrooms being shouted at by House Captains, now the whole experience seems rose-tinted, perhaps it is because of the way that our house bonded in the adversity of the 100th rendition of a song. Perhaps it is because of the excitement of the final performance where all the work paid off in the dancing, singing and costumes. As a non-musical, non-performing arts student I would never have been involved in this sort of performance if it hadn't been compulsory, but I am so glad it was. Never did I feel more like a Wally girl than when watching my last House Music Competition, sympathising with the stress the House Captains were radiating as they waved their lyric prompts and joining in the battle to drown out other House chants with "ch-ch-chchch-chchchch- Chartwell!"

"Very quickly at Wally I realised that participation was definitely a key part of a Wally education and now I love the passionate debates in American History between the Nixon lovers and haters as Mrs Joynes tries to keep us vaguely on topic. Wally has given me confidence to be myself."

Charlotte Whittaker, Classics at Trinity Hall, Cambridge

"Although each and every one of us will be sad to go, Wally has been fundamental in creating friendships which will long outlive our time here."

Jessica Clayton, History at Sheffield

"My favourite club at Wally has been Elite Swimming. Although it is hard, especially in winter, to drag myself out of bed and into school at a very unreasonable hour it is ALWAYS WORTH IT. Braving the cold water at 7.30 am is made so much easier by the gorgeous pool."

Ciara Dickson, applying for Psychology following a gap year

"My most memorable Wally play was *Nicholas Nickleby*. I played the character of Fanny Squeers. I dressed up completely disgustingly, wore a matted ginger wig, blacked out my teeth and made my eyes red and tired. I got to put on a crazy Yorkshire accent and act with no inhibitions."

Ella Lane, History at Bristol

"One of my favourite memories of being at Wally Hall has to be the interaction between the year groups and the friendly environment in which we spent every day.

The pyjama party, which we Sixth Formers organised for the Year 7s, was hilarious with each girl becoming more and more competitive trying to win the chocolate game, their little chocolate-smothered faces beaming up at the Sixth Formers, worn out after a tough game of gladiators."

Olivia Haswell, Art Foundation at Maidstone

Voices from 2013 - Senior School diary extracts

"On January 21st 2013, after a heavy snowfall, we woke up to a Snow Day. We were provided with some work on the website, through the student login pages so that we didn't fall too far behind in our work... The next day school reopened and we returned to Wally, finding, with much amusement, that two mysterious snowmen, complete with hats and scarves, had appeared on two of the benches, one outside the Science Block and one by the Hub."

"The day started off with Prayers, which Mrs Milner leads. After the hymn she read us a story with a moral in it and then she read out all the notices. Next it was time for our first lesson of Art. We are learning different stitches and we are going to stitch a painting of sweets. Firstly, I ironed my sweets picture, which I had put paint on. Because the colours were quite faint I had to outline the sweets in pencil, using the light box."

"This past week has been exciting but very stressful as I have been putting on a devised comedy with my Drama class. We are a group of five and our performance is a comic spoof of James Bond. I am playing some hilarious characters, including the Queen."

"In English we are studying *Much Ado About Nothing* and we focused on exercises using dramatic monologues and pairing old English with modern language. The bell then rang for lunch which was rice with chicken in a lovely lemon and coriander sauce. And for dessert, berry smoothie and shortbread. I then went to a "Strictly Wally" practice, ready for the auditions on Friday."

"This term in Swimming we have been looking at lifesaving. We have tried out some of the ways to save people's lives. After our warm-up we tried throwing rope in groups of four. We had to shout to the casualty, throw the rope and then pull them to the side. In Music we are learning about the blues. We watched a short video on the whiteboard in which people in Africa were telling us how this music originated. The lyrics are based on sad things in your life that you want to put into the past."

"When we were nearly at the end of our Physics lesson we went to the ICT suite and used a website we had never used before to learn about "moments". After a long and busy lesson it was Break time. At Break we have different types of snacks each day. We have caramels, Marylands, Kit Kats, shortbreads and Digestives. After Break, it was time for the dreaded Maths test."

"In Chemistry we are learning about the reactivity series of metals and today we were lucky enough to do an experiment. Our teacher set up three experiments showing different metals in acid. One metal turned sparkly, one had crystals and one went blue!"

"In Gym we have been doing travelling, balancing and flying (off boxes and benches). Today we had to present the routine we had been practising for around two weeks and we had lots of good gymnastic ability and flying in the class."

"The Houses started to prepare for House Music with rehearsals in our house rooms becoming more frequent. The theme for 2013 is Decades, with Houses each being assigned a decade from the '60s through to 2010. The House Captains and other members of the UVI choose two songs, one for the whole House to perform and one for a smaller ensemble group."

"After P.E. we had to run up the Erasmus stairs to make sure we were in time for History, where we were learning about King Edward and the changes he made when he was on the throne. It was then time for Break and we went down to the Maths Block to chat a little before it was time for the lesson."

Voices from 2013 - Junior School Diary Extracts

"On Friday my school Walthamstow Hall had a pink day. We all had to dress in pink and bring in one pound if we wanted to wear something pink. The reason we were doing this is because of a charity called Because I Am a Girl, which helps girls all around the globe to have an education like ours that will help them get a good job. The night before Pink Day I looked through my crowded wardrobe and found a pair of bright pink boots, some pink tracksuit bottoms, a light pink top and a jumper."

"I think lunchtimes at school are great. On Thursday there is normally a roast dinner, on Fridays there is fish and chips, and on Wednesdays, sometimes we have pizza. Sometimes we have treacle tart, ice cream, fruit salad or Eton Mess. They are all scrumptious but I have to say that treacle tart is the best for me! At break times there is always someone to play with and there are lots of toys such as balls, hoops and stilts in the playground."

"On Thursday it was World Book Day. I dressed as Dorothy from *The Wizard of Oz*. We had a very special assembly when we walked up on stage, class by class, and said who we were."

"Our School Council is a group of pupils who meet to discuss issues relating to school life. I am the representative for my class and they voted me on to the Council. I had to give a speech to get chosen. I was excited to be chosen and a bit proud too!"

"In February I broke my finger playing Netball. This is a sport where you pass a ball down the court and aim to score a goal. I broke my finger when the ball flew towards me and I jumped at the same time as somebody on the opposite team. I heard a horrible crack and I almost screamed. That afternoon I was not allowed to play in a match against Granville."

Walthamstow Hall whole-school photograph, 2013

Bibliography

Walthamstow Hall School Archives.

Written histories of the school:

Elsie Pike and Constance Curryer
*The Story of Walthamstow Hall Part 1:
1838 – 1938* Longmore Press Ltd. 1938

U.K.Moore
*The Story of Walthamstow Hall Part 2:
1938 – 1970* Longmore Press Ltd. 1973

Audrey Third and Anne Evans
The Story of Walthamstow Hall 1968 – 1989

Helen Hook and Diane Hurst (compilers)
The Ship's Log 1989

Ann Vaughan
The Story of Walthamstow Hall 1990 – 2002

Other sources:

Avery, Gillian.
The Best Type of Girl Deutsch 1991

Ed. Aveling, The Rev Thomas
The Missionary Souvenir John Snow, Houlston
and Stoneman, Ward and Co. 1850

Bosworth, George
*Some More Walthamstow Houses and their
Interesting Associations* (no date)

Budden, H.D.
*The Story of Marsh Street Congregational
Church* Bobby and Co. Ltd. 1923

Cathcart Borer, Mary
Willingly to School Lutterworth 1976

Dunscliff, Joy
A Rude Awakening self-published, no date

Evans, Brian
Bygone Walthamstow Phillimore & Co Ltd.
1995

Hollybush Residents Association
Hollybush on the Map 1999

Kamm, Josephine
Hope Deferred Methuen 1965

Mander, David
Walthamstow Past Historical Publications Ltd.
2001

Reaney, P.H.
A History of Walthamstow OUP 1981

Robinson, Jane
Bluestockings Viking 2009

Spencer Clark, William
The Suburban Homes of London
Chatto and Windus 1881

Ed. WGS Tonkin
*The Record of Walthamstow Antiquarian
Society* (date not known)

Waltham Forest Archive

Walthamstow Antiquarian Society
Report 1933

Wilkins, Joyce
A Child's Eye View 1904 – 1920
The Book Guild Ltd. 1992

600 YEARS IN THE MAKING

Highlights from the Museum Collections of the
University of St Andrews

DR HELEN C. RAWSON

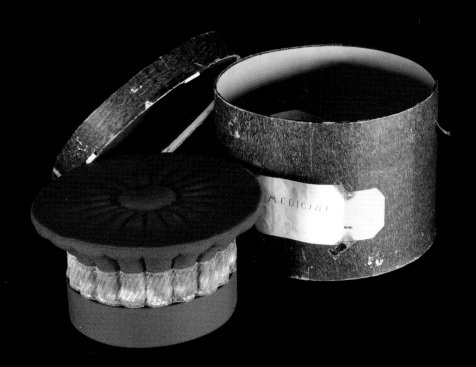

Published in Great Britain in 2016 by Shire Publications Ltd (part of Bloomsbury Publishing Plc),
PO Box 883, Oxford, OX1 9PL, UK.
PO Box 3985, New York, NY 10185-3985, USA.
E-mail: shire@shirebooks.co.uk
www.shirebooks.co.uk

ISBN-13: 9781784420321
PDF e-book ISBN: 9781784421618
ePub ISBN: 9781784421625

Typeset in Candara and Garamond Premier Pro
Index by Alison Worthington
Printed in China through World Print Ltd.
16 17 18 19 20   10 9 8 7 6 5 4 3 2 1

Image acknowledgements

Cover image: 'Great Astrolabe', 1575, made by Humphrey Cole of London.

Title page: Sample Medicine cap, Bosc of Paris, about 1868.

Photography on cover and pages 1, 5, 6, 7, 9, 15, 21, 22, 23, 29, 32-5, 38, 39, 41, 42, 47, 49, 54,
55, 60 and 61 by Scriptura. All other images are from the collection of the University of St
Andrews.

Shire Publications supports the Woodland Trust, the UK's leading woodland conservation
charity. Between 2014 and 2018 our donations will be spent on their Centenary Woods project
in the UK.

Contents

Foreword

Founded between 1410 and 1414, the University of St Andrews is the oldest university in Scotland, and the third most ancient in the English-speaking world (after Oxford and Cambridge). The Museum Collections of the University of St Andrews consist of about 115,000 artefacts and specimens acquired throughout its 600-year history. This short guidebook highlights items which, while interesting, celebrated or significant in their own right, reflect the richness and diversity of the wider collections.

Some items now in the museum collections are connected to the history and traditions of the University. The magnificent medieval maces have been used in ceremonies since the 15th century, as they still are at graduation and other events today. They provide a direct connection to the experiences of past generations of students and staff: an unbroken link from the University's earliest days to the present time. Furniture, such as the elaborate St Andrews Cupboard from the early 1500s, medieval carved stones, portraits and stained glass have also passed down through the centuries. Academic dress, silver drinking vessels and relics of sports and pastimes contained within the Heritage Collection offer insights into the changing life of the University and its colleges over the past 600 years.

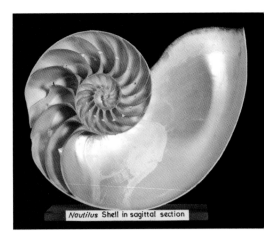

Nautilus Shell in sagittal section

Other items were originally acquired for teaching and research purposes. These include intricate scientific instruments, of which the earliest were probably purchased by James Gregory, Professor of Mathematics, in his attempt to establish the first purpose-built observatory in the British Isles in St Andrews in the early 1670s. Today the Collection of Historic Scientific Instruments contains over 1000 items reflecting five centuries of scientific breakthroughs and discoveries: when new, many represented cutting-edge technology. The Chemistry Collection ranges from rare and fragile examples of early glassware to specimens such as the remarkable samples of around 900 sugars, the structures of which were identified by Professors Purdie and Irvine in the 20th century. Like the Heritage Collection, the Chemistry and Historic Scientific Instrument Collections are Recognised Collections of National Significance, indicating their importance to Scottish history, life and culture, as well as their international renown.

Ethnographic and archaeological artefacts, some of which were once displayed amid a collection of 'curiosities' shown to visitors to the University Library in the 18th century, offer insights into human history and cultures, both within Scotland and around the globe. Zoological and geological specimens enable exploration and understanding of the natural world, while the Anatomy and Pathology Collection represents developments in medicine and human health.

The art holdings, including the strong collection of contemporary Scottish art, represent the creative impulses also present in many other fields, including the sciences. Diverse, beautiful, startling or fascinating, the varied and still developing museum collections reflect not only the history of the University of St Andrews, and the discoveries made by its staff and students, but its interaction with and influence in the wider world.

I hope that this brief guidebook will intrigue and inspire you, and encourage you to explore the museum collections further.

Dr Helen C. Rawson
Co-Director, Museum Collections Unit
February 2016

Mary Queen of Scots at Fotheringhay *by John Duncan, 1929 (left)*

Nautilus *shell (above)*

Discovering the Museum Collections

The main museum venue is MUSA, the Museum of the University of St Andrews, established in 2008. MUSA has several galleries exploring University life and history, and key discoveries and innovations connected to St Andrews. There is an education centre, the 'Learning Loft', and a viewing terrace with a spectacular outlook over St Andrews Bay.

A wide-ranging programme of temporary exhibitions is held throughout the year: the website gives up-to-date listings and venues. The zoology collections are displayed in the Bell Pettigrew Museum, a rare and fascinating survival of an Edwardian teaching museum, open to the public at regular times during the University's summer vacation.

Not all the museum collections, including some of those featured in this guidebook, are on display at any one time. However, all can be seen by advance appointment, usually in the MUSA Collections Centre, an open-access store and research centre where regular 'behind-the-scenes' tours of the stored collections are held.

The collections are used to support teaching and research in the University. The curators also run a busy schools programme and a varied public events programme, ranging from gallery tours and formal lectures to family and children's activities, geology walks, science festivals, art workshops, and music and poetry recitals. All museum venues, and most events, are free of charge. Please see the website for details of opening times, exhibitions and events listings.

st-andrews.ac.uk/museum

Mouth ornament, Papua New Guinea (above)

Tray of butterflies (right)

History and Development of the Museum Collections

The University of St Andrews was founded in stages between 1410 and 1414. Despite the poverty of the University in its first years, one of the earliest acts of the Faculty of Arts, on 17 January 1416, was to commission a costly silver mace. This mace represented the authority of the Faculty and of the University, and publicly proclaimed their status. Still in use today, at graduation and other ceremonial events, it was the first item in the University's artefact collections. The three 15th-century maces – the Arts Mace, the Mace of the Faculty of Canon Law (about 1450) and the Mace of St Salvator's College (1461) – arguably remain the most important, for their beauty,

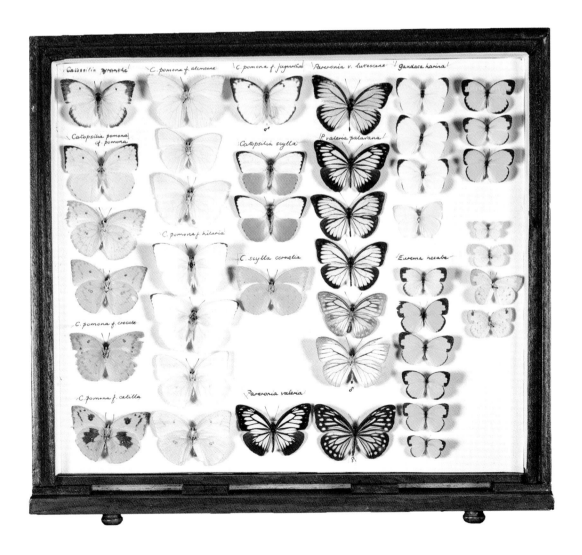

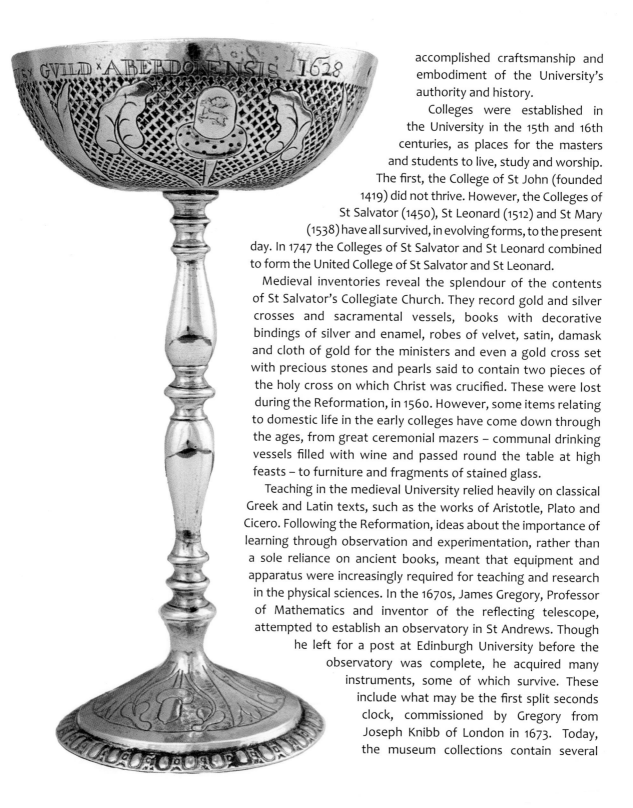

accomplished craftsmanship and embodiment of the University's authority and history.

Colleges were established in the University in the 15th and 16th centuries, as places for the masters and students to live, study and worship. The first, the College of St John (founded 1419) did not thrive. However, the Colleges of St Salvator (1450), St Leonard (1512) and St Mary (1538) have all survived, in evolving forms, to the present day. In 1747 the Colleges of St Salvator and St Leonard combined to form the United College of St Salvator and St Leonard.

Medieval inventories reveal the splendour of the contents of St Salvator's Collegiate Church. They record gold and silver crosses and sacramental vessels, books with decorative bindings of silver and enamel, robes of velvet, satin, damask and cloth of gold for the ministers and even a gold cross set with precious stones and pearls said to contain two pieces of the holy cross on which Christ was crucified. These were lost during the Reformation, in 1560. However, some items relating to domestic life in the early colleges have come down through the ages, from great ceremonial mazers – communal drinking vessels filled with wine and passed round the table at high feasts – to furniture and fragments of stained glass.

Teaching in the medieval University relied heavily on classical Greek and Latin texts, such as the works of Aristotle, Plato and Cicero. Following the Reformation, ideas about the importance of learning through observation and experimentation, rather than a sole reliance on ancient books, meant that equipment and apparatus were increasingly required for teaching and research in the physical sciences. In the 1670s, James Gregory, Professor of Mathematics and inventor of the reflecting telescope, attempted to establish an observatory in St Andrews. Though he left for a post at Edinburgh University before the observatory was complete, he acquired many instruments, some of which survive. These include what may be the first split seconds clock, commissioned by Gregory from Joseph Knibb of London in 1673. Today, the museum collections contain several

Guild Cup, London, 1613–14 (above)

Puffer fish (right)

centuries' worth of instruments and teaching apparatus in the fields of mathematics, physics, astronomy, chemistry and more recently, psychology, representing developments in technology and human understanding of the physical world.

The same desire to explore and understand the wider world led to the formation of a collection of 'curiosities' in the University Library from about 1700. These were kept with the books, like them tools for investigation, discovery and comprehension. The 'curiosities' ranged from natural history specimens to ethnographic and archaeological artefacts representing diverse cultures across the globe. The natural history specimens tended to be acquired for their unusual or exotic nature (at least to 18th-century Scots). Like many cabinets of curiosities, the collection at St Andrews included corals, which seemed to have both plant- and mineral-like qualities, a bezoar (a stone found within human or animal bodies) and petrified specimens or fossils. The ethnographic objects included many domestic items, such as gourds and the remarkable North American Algonquin birch bark basket acquired in the early 1700s which still survives in the collections today. There was an Egyptian mummy (of which only the head and a foot remain), a hammock, a war canoe, and snow shoes from Canada. Also displayed were weapons from different cultures, used for hunting and fighting. The period during which the Library collection was formed, the 18th and early 19th centuries, saw the rapid expansion of British overseas territories and the formation of the British Empire. The display of weapons taken from subject nations, presented in the Library with a bust of George III, reflected the impact of the British imperial project, as well as interest in the cultures represented.

In 1838 the University and the Literary and Philosophical Society of St Andrews jointly established a formal museum in the United College buildings, to which the 'curiosities' were transferred. The collections, in the fields of anatomy, botany, geology, zoology, coins, archaeology and ethnography, were systematically categorised and arranged by subject area. The museum was used to support teaching and research, and was open to the public, for a charge, at specific hours. Donations poured in, from friends and alumni of the University working across the world, including birds from Australia, Chinese insects and Indian minerals, as well as marine specimens presented by St Andrews fishermen and local archaeological material. In 1904, the Literary and Philosophical Society, which was in decline, transferred its interest in the collections to the University.

By the early 20th century, the collections had outgrown their home in the United College. In 1912 they were transferred to the purpose-built Bell Pettigrew Museum in the University's Bute medical buildings. The construction of the museum was funded by Elsie Bell Pettigrew in memory of her husband James, late Professor of Medicine. The museum served the university and town until the 1950s, when it underwent a period of decline. The space was reduced in size, and though the zoology collections remained on display, as they do there today, the other material was transferred to University departments to which its subject matter related.

During the 1990s, a professional curatorial team and museum service were established. MUSA, the Museum of the University of St Andrews, was opened in 2008. New stores were established in 2010, including the MUSA Collections Centre, an open-access store and research centre, where the collections not on display can be seen by appointment. Today the thriving museum service supports teaching and research in the University, including the postgraduate Museum Studies degree, as well as providing programmes for schools, and events and activities for the local community and other visitors.

Transit theodolite by William Cary, late 18th–early 19th century (above)

Terrestrial globe by J. & W. Cary, 1806 (right)

Seal of Authority

Matrix of the University Seal, 1414–18, and its impression

The University of St Andrews is Scotland's oldest university, founded between 1410 and 1414. It was a pioneering institution, allowing Scots to study at university level within their own country for the first time.

Religious and political tensions in Europe in the early 15th century made it difficult for Scottish students to attend foreign universities as they had previously, mainly in France and England. The Great Schism in the Papacy, when rival popes were established in Rome and Avignon, divided Europe, with England, Italy and Germany supporting the Roman popes, and Scotland, France and Spain the Avignon line. When France abandoned its support for the Avignon pope Benedict XIII in 1408, some Scots students returned home.

The process of establishing the University of St Andrews began in 1410, when a group of masters set up a school of higher studies in the city. In February 1412 Henry Wardlaw, Bishop of St Andrews, granted it a charter of incorporation. The final stage in founding a medieval university was to receive authorisation from the Pope, and application was made to Benedict XIII in Peñiscola, Aragon (now Spain) in the name of the Church and of the King and Estates of Scotland. On 28 August 1413, Pope Benedict XIII issued six Bulls, or charters, granting the institution in St Andrews university status and establishing its rights and privileges. After an arduous journey over medieval roads and the sea, these arrived in St Andrews on 3 February 1414. The foundation of Scotland's first university was celebrated with the ringing of church bells, a service of thanksgiving in the Cathedral and bonfires in the streets.

The matrix for the University seal was cast about the time of the University's foundation, between 1414 and 1418. Pressed into melted wax, the matrix creates a reverse impression, or seal, which was used to authenticate important documents. The seal shows St Andrew on his cross. The figures below represent either a master lecturing to a class of students, or a formal university meeting. The crouching figure holds a light, or perhaps a mace. Above are the arms of the University's founders, Bishop Wardlaw (left on matrix, right on seal), Pope Benedict XIII (centre), and King James I.

University Seal matrix (right)
Brass; 8.0 cm diameter
St Andrews University Library, Special Collections, UYUY103

University Seal, attached to Master of Arts diploma granted to Thomas James, 1626 (left)
St Andrews University Library, Special Collections, UYUY348

Examination and Celebration

Blackstone, about 1420

Birretum, 1696

T his apparently benign object will have been the cause of a good deal of trepidation in students over the centuries. From about 1420 until the 18th century, candidates for the Master of Arts degree sat on the blackstone for their oral examination. Here, they were questioned by the examiners, with particular importance being attached to their skills in disputation, or debating. If successful, students in the medieval period were expected to present gloves and caps to their teachers, and entertain them to a sumptuous banquet.

On achieving the Master of Arts degree, each student was ceremonially 'capped' by the Chancellor, as students are still in the modern graduation ceremony. The birretum, or cap, now used in this ceremony was made for the University in 1696, for the graduation of John Arbuthnot, the first identifiable graduate in medicine. Sadly it is not, as legend has it, made from John Knox's breeches! The moment when a student is capped – touched on the head with the birretum – and graduates, provides a tangible and personal link to those who have passed through the University before.

To us, the students of the Middle Ages would have seemed very young, entering the University aged about thirteen. They were all male: women were not allowed to study at the University until the late 19th century. They lived under close supervision in the colleges.

Statutes dated 1544 tell us about life in St Leonard's College. Students had to rise at 5 am in summer and 5.30 am in winter. Mass was usually said at 6 am, and lessons began at 7 am. Students were forbidden to wear fashionable clothes and coloured caps. They could not leave the college without special permission. They had to speak in Latin at all times and help with domestic work. Once a week, they were allowed to play sport, but 'dishonest and dangerous' games, such as football and dice, were banned.

Though the lives of students have changed dramatically since the early years of the University, the forbidding blackstone, hewn from basalt, and the equally plain birretum, remind us of the constants of the student experience: the pressure of exams and the celebration of graduation.

Blackstone (right)
Basalt; 41.5 × 49.0 × 49.0 cm
HC825

Birretum (left)
Cotton (?); 35.0 cm diameter

The Thistle and the Rose

St Andrews Cupboard, early 1500s

This magnificent oak cupboard dates from the early 16th century. While the sides are decorated with delicate linenfold panelling, vines and foliage sprout vigorously across the twelve panels on the front. Among the stylised leaves and clusters of grapes can be found, by those who search carefully, three flowers: a thistle, a rose and a marguerite (daisy).

When and how the cupboard first came to the University is not precisely known, though it has been here for many centuries. Although inventories of the furniture of the early colleges survive, including one of the bedchambers of St Leonard's College taken in 1544, the descriptions are not detailed enough to allow individual surviving pieces to be identified.

The clue to the cupboard's origins may lie in the three flowers among the lush and fruitful foliage. The thistle and rose have long held symbolical importance as the flowers of Scotland and England. In 1503 James IV, King of Scotland married Margaret Tudor, sister of King Henry VIII of England. The thistle, rose and marguerite, for Margaret, appear conspicuously in the decoration of the ratification of their marriage contract, dated 17th December 1502, illuminated at Stirling by the court painter Thomas Galbraith. The same flowers appear in a Book of Hours commissioned by James IV as a wedding gift for his bride.

St Leonard's College was established in 1512, with James IV confirming the foundation charter in February 1513. This cupboard may honour that association, being either a royal gift, or a college commission in honour of their patron. The fertile vines symbolise the health and richness of the kingdom of Scotland under the royal couple.

St Andrews Cupboard (right) and detail (left)
Oak; 221.0 × 155.5 × 59.0 cm
HC839

Drinking Together

St Mary's College Mazer, about 1562

St Leonard's College Mazer, mid-16th–early 17th century

A mazer is a communal drinking cup, usually with a wooden bowl, often made of maple wood. In the 16th century standing mazers, in which the bowl is supported on a silver foot and stem, and is perhaps decorated with a silver or silver gilt rim and ornate cover, were fashionable status symbols, owned by noble families, guilds and colleges. Today, just nine Scottish standing mazers survive, two from the medieval colleges of the University of St Andrews.

The mazer of St Mary's College was made in Edinburgh by Alexander Auchinleck, probably in 1562. It has a silver foot and rim. The decorated silver print at the centre of the wooden bowl is inscribed with the date 1562, two biblical texts in Latin, and the words 'COLLEGIV * NOVVM * SCTE * ADREE', or 'New College St Andrews', a common name for St Mary's College in this period. It bears the mark of Thomas Ewing, who was responsible for testing the quality of Edinburgh silverwork. It is the oldest known fully hallmarked piece of Edinburgh silver.

The St Leonard's College mazer is unusual in that it has a silver bowl, which may have replaced an earlier wooden one. In its original form, it probably dates from between the mid-16th and early 17th centuries.

The mazers would have been passed round the college table ceremonially at great feasts. Each of the three colleges of the University of St Andrews owned fine silver and gold vessels, presented by patrons or former students. Ostentatiously displayed, shining in the candlelight, as part of the fabric and ritual of formal dining, the magnificent and costly wares would impress students and visitors alike with the prestige, authority and time-honoured traditions of the colleges. The handing round of the great mazers from person to person for ceremonial drinking was designed to foster a collegial spirit and reinforce loyalties and participation in college life, helped along with plentiful libations of wine or ale.

St Mary's College Mazer (right)
Silver and maple wood; H 16.0, bowl diameter 22.8 cm
HC292

St Leonard's College Mazer (left)
Silver and silver gilt; H 19.1, bowl diameter 23.8 cm
HC261

Seat of Power

Parliament Chair, mid-1660s

The Lower Hall or Parliament Hall (from the West) circa 1643–1700, by G. H. Bushnell, mid-20th century

D uring the winter of 1645–46, plague in Scotland's major cities brought the Scottish Parliament to St Andrews. The Parliament met in the University's new 'public school', completed in 1643 and known afterwards as Parliament Hall. This oak chair is, by tradition, said to have been used by the Presiding Officer. It is a grand piece, decorated with stylised flowers and scrolls.

The University's 'public school' was the only large gathering place in St Andrews, with the exception of the Town Church. It consisted of a spacious hall, used for University meetings, disputations (formal debates) and ceremonies and, occasionally, as an exercise room for students. Above it was the University Library. The hall and library were proudly shown to visitors, including the writer Daniel Defoe, who travelled round Scotland in the early 18th century, and John Macky, who described the hall in detail in *A Journey Through Scotland* (London, 1723). From these accounts and the University records George Herbert Bushnell, the University Librarian, was able to reconstruct the appearance of the room about the time the Parliament gathered.

The Parliament met in St Andrews during the Civil War, a period of power struggles and shifting allegiances. Important royalist prisoners, captured at the Battle of Philiphaugh, were tried and condemned to death at this Parliament. They were executed close by, in Market Street. Among those beheaded was Sir Robert Spottiswood, formerly President of the Court of Session and Secretary of State of Scotland. Spottiswood had aggrieved the University, which after his execution petitioned Parliament for his books, claiming that it was notoriously known that both he and his father, Archbishop Spottiswood, had borrowed books from the Library and not returned them. The petition was granted. This tells us something of the importance and value of books in this period, and perhaps also of the long memories of librarians for overdue volumes.

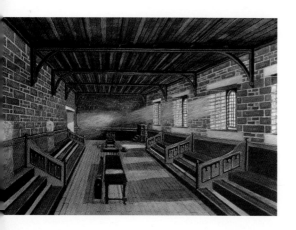

Parliament Chair (right)
Oak; 111.0 × 62.5 × 57.5 cm
HC790

The Lower Hall or Parliament Hall (from the West) circa 1643–1700 *(left)*
Watercolour on paper; 25.2 × 37.5 cm
HC507

Observing the Skies

'Great Astrolabe', 1575, and Universal Instrument, 1582, made by Humphrey Cole of London

On 10 June 1673 the University issued a commission to James Gregory, the first Regius Professor of Mathematics (1668–74), to go to London and purchase 'such instruments and utensils as he, with the advice of other skilful persons, shall judge most necessary and usefull' for equipping a new observatory for the University. The creation of an observatory in St Andrews was a significant and extremely expensive undertaking. Had it been completed, it would have been the first purpose-built observatory in the British Isles. As the commission declared, it was intended to improve teaching and research in 'naturall philosophy and the Mathematicall sciences' and allow 'observations on the heavens and other bodys of this universe', enabling the University 'to keep correspondence with learned and inquisitive persons every where'. At a time when understanding of the universe was advancing rapidly, the observatory and instruments would allow the University to be at the forefront of intellectual debate.

Gregory was well qualified to establish an observatory. Inventor of the reflecting telescope and a member of the new Royal Society in London, he had studied at Padua University (where Galileo had earlier taught) and was familiar with recent advances in the mathematical sciences and with Continental observatories. Seeking the advice of John Flamsteed, later the first Astronomer Royal at Greenwich (founded 1675), he purchased many instruments, and obtained others from powerful patrons.

The 'Great Astrolabe' and universal instrument pictured here are prestigious instruments. They were made by Humphrey Cole, the most eminent Elizabethan instrument maker, who equipped Martin Frobisher's voyage in search of the north-west passage in 1576. Dating from nearly a century before the observatory, they may have been purchased by Gregory through the thriving second-hand instrument market in London, or donated by a wealthy nobleman. Both could be used for navigation and astronomical observation. The size and beauty of the astrolabe suggests it was designed for decorative as well as practical use, perhaps in an aristocratic household.

The observatory seems never to have been brought into full working use. Gregory's radical scientific teachings were not welcomed by all his colleagues, who found their more old-fashioned theories mocked by his students. Discouraged, he left St Andrews for a professorship at Edinburgh University in 1674, taking his expertise but leaving many splendid instruments.

'Great Astrolabe' (right)
Brass; 61.0 cm diameter
PH201

Universal Instrument (left)
Brass; H 44.5 × 36.0 cm diameter
PH203

Sporting Glory

Silver Arrow archery competition arrows and medals, 1618 to mid-1750s

'By luck not skill'; 'Nothing is so difficult that skill will not conquer'; 'Great Apollo grants this first honour to you and does not begrudge weapons matching his'; 'Victory will not stop here'; 'The Leslies are accustomed to win their first crown of victory from this source'; 'Our triumphs are without killing'; 'Unexpected victor'. These Latin inscriptions, modest, boastful, learned, philosophical or demonstrating family pride, are engraved on a remarkable series of medals created over a period of 140 years.

The Silver Arrow competition was an annual event to find the champion student archer. Organised by the Faculty of Arts, the competitors were students of St Salvator's and St Leonard's Colleges. The winner was awarded the honour of commissioning a silver medal to mark his victory, at his own expense. These were attached to silver arrows and paraded down to the archery range at the Bow Butts for the competition each year, a merry and lively affair. In 1628, when James Graham, later 1st Marquis of Montrose, won, he paid for a drummer and piper to announce the contest, and for supper for all the archers.

Three silver arrows and 70 medals survive. Each medal has the figure of an archer on one side and, usually, the coat of arms of the victor on the other. Each is unique, and in their size, design and inscription, which was often selected from classical sources such as Virgil, the medals reflect the wealth, status, character and learning of the victor. Several winners were to become prominent figures in Scottish history: Montrose was Captain General of the Royalist forces in Scotland during the Civil War.

There are gaps in the sequence of medals, particularly between 1630 and 1675, the troubled period of the Covenanting movement and the Civil War, when perhaps the competition did not take place. Some champions may not have been wealthy enough to commission medals. Between 1676 and 1707, these grew to an enormous size as the victors competed to present ever more elaborate and costly medals, until the University imposed a weight limit. The competition died out in the 1750s, not long after the union of St Salvator's and St Leonard's Colleges in 1747, perhaps because the spur of collegiate rivalry had gone.

Medal of John, Lord Leslie, 1694. Became 9th Earl of Rothes (top)
Silver; 19.7 × 14.7 cm
HC814(27)

Medal of Francis Murray, Lord Doune, c. 1754. Became 8th Earl of Moray (bottom)
Silver; 9.2 × 8.7 cm
HC814(70)
The St Andrews skyline features.

Murder and Intrigue

The Death of Archbishop Sharpe by John Opie, 1797
Portrait of Archbishop Sharp by Sir Peter Lely, about 1666

O n 3 May 1679 James Sharp, Archbishop of St Andrews and Chancellor of the University, was travelling home by carriage to St Andrews with his daughter Isabella. As they reached Magus Muir, to the west of the town, a shot was fired at Sharp. He was forced out of the carriage and, before his horrified daughter, hacked to death by a number of local lairds and farmers.

Sharp's assailants were extremist Presbyterians, covenanters who opposed Episcopalian practices in the church, including the government of the church by a hierarchy of bishops, and the interference of the state in church affairs. Tensions had begun some decades earlier. In 1603, Scotland and England were united under one monarch, as James VI of Scotland inherited the English throne from Elizabeth I, becoming James I of England. Attempts by James VI / I and his son Charles I to impose English religious practices on Scotland outraged many Scots and were interpreted as an attack on their national and religious identity. In 1638 the National Covenant was drawn up in protest, asserting Scotland's rights in matters of church and state. Conflict continued throughout the mid-1600s.

In 1661 Sharp was appointed Archbishop of St Andrews by Charles II and attempted to destroy Presbyterianism and Covenanting principles. As he had formerly been a prominent Presbyterian minister, entrusted by the Scottish kirk to represent its views to the king, Presbyterians saw this as a betrayal of their cause. This dramatic work by John Opie, painted in 1797, emphasises the violence of Sharp's last moments and the desperation of his daughter, who survived. It was engraved and published as a print in David Hume's *The History of England*. It was bought by the University in 2008 with support from the National Fund for Acquisitions, the Art Fund, the Binks Trust and a private donor.

A contemporary portrait of Sharp by Sir Peter Lely, Principal Painter to Charles II, was acquired by the University in 1950 for just £26.5s. Long thought to be a copy of a lost work by Lely, conservation work in the 1990s revealed its true quality, while research established its provenance.

The Death of Archbishop Sharpe *(right)*
Oil on canvas; 224.8 × 174.0 cm
HC2008.9

Portrait of Archbishop Sharp (left)
Oil on canvas; 124.9 × 101.2 cm
HC225

From a New World

Bark Basket, early 1700s

From about 1700, a variety of objects, which would later in the century be collectively known as 'the Curiosities', began to be held and displayed in the University Library. These were items of interest to the curious and enquiring mind, kept among the scholarly texts, and like them, full of potential for research, knowledge and understanding. During the 18th century, the collection grew steadily, with zoological, botanical and geological specimens offering new insights into the natural world; and archaeological and ethnographic artefacts, from cultures across the globe, illuminating human history.

The period during which the collection developed, the 18th and first half of the 19th centuries, saw the rapid expansion of overseas territories and the formation of the British Empire. Former students of the University travelled abroad, in the military, as administrators in the civil service, and as missionaries and explorers, spreading across the world and sending home to their university the interesting things that they found. Back came specimens from India, Burma, Sri Lanka, Malaysia, Indonesia, Madagascar, New Guinea, New Zealand, China, various parts of Africa, North, Central and South America, and other countries besides. These included a mummy from Egypt, sculptures of deities from India, and in 1792 a 'spear of wood' from the Sandwich Islands (Hawaii), which had first been mapped by Captain James Cook only 14 years previously.

This remarkable bark basket arrived in St Andrews in 1728. It is from North America, of Algonquin origin. It was probably made by the Cree people of the Hudson Bay or James Bay area of what is now Canada, and was used for collecting and storing food. It is made from a single piece of birch bark stitched together with spruce root and decorated with porcupine quills.

Bark Basket
Birch bark, spruce root, porcupine quills; 9.0 × 22.3 × 24.5 cm
ET1977.125

Seeing Further

Reflecting telescope made by James Short of Edinburgh, 1736

In February 1676 Isaac Newton, who was to become renowned for formulating the theory of gravity and for defining the laws of motion and attraction, declared in a letter to Robert Hooke:

If I have seen further, it is by standing on the shoulders of giants.

He was acknowledging the work of earlier figures in the history of science, such as Copernicus and Galileo: without their insights, he implied, he could not have made his own discoveries.

The late 17th century was a time when men of science literally were enabling the world to see further. Robert Hooke's experiments with microscopes led to the publication, in 1665, of *Micrographia*, a volume containing illustrations and descriptions of the structure of minute organisms and objects, including a flea, a gnat and plant cells. In *Optica Promota* (1663) James Gregory gave the first description of a reflecting telescope. Through a combination of lenses and mirrors, the reflecting telescope would allow greater magnification to be obtained with barrels of shorter length than was possible with the standard refracting telescope, which lacked mirrors. Some of the earlier refracting telescopes were of immense length. During his time as the first Regius Professor of Mathematics at the University (1668–74), Gregory had contemplated buying one 100 feet long. Although instrument makers took some time to master the specialist process, in the 18th century the 'Gregorian' reflecting telescope became the standard form.

The telescope pictured here is of the pattern invented by James Gregory, in which an image of the object, produced by reflection from two concave metal mirrors, is viewed through an eyepiece lens set in the centre of the main mirror. It was ordered by the University in 1736 from James Short, the outstanding telescope maker of his day, and cost 25 guineas. It was the largest telescope Short had yet made and was suitable for serious astronomical observation. Short made improvements to this telescope in 1741 and again in 1749, adding apparatus allowing the planets and some of the stars to be found in daylight. This telescope was cutting-edge scientific equipment.

Reflecting telescope
24-inch focus, 4.5 inch aperture
Brass, wood, glass; 51.0 × 94.0 × 46.0 cm
PH206

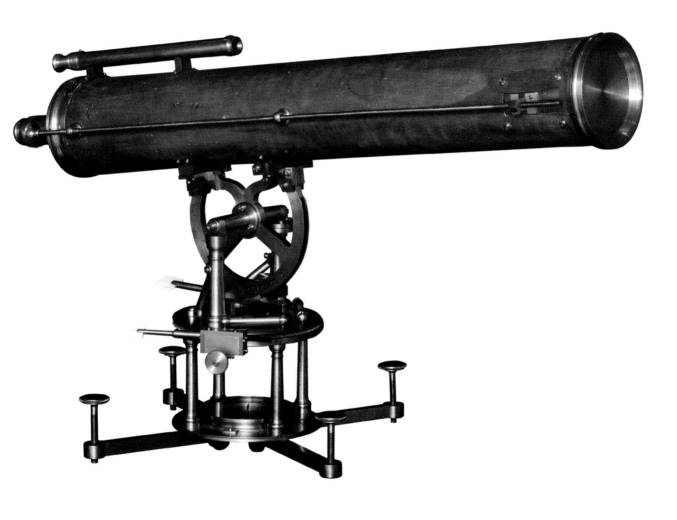

Power and Ceremony

Mace of the Faculty of Arts, 1416–19
Mace of the Faculty of Canon Law, about 1450
Mace of St Salvator's College, 1461

I n its early years, the University of St Andrews was an impoverished institution. Until 1419, it had no buildings of its own. Lectures took place in the Priory or the private rooms of the masters, while the masters and students lodged wherever they could obtain space. Books and other necessities of all kinds were in short supply and money scarce. Despite this, one of the earliest acts of the Faculty of Arts, on 17 January 1416, was to commission a magnificent and expensive mace. So important was the acquisition of a mace that, in May 1416, even money set aside for books was diverted to fund it.

Maces are emblems of authority, status, wealth and power. Owned by the older Continental universities, they were carried ceremonially in procession in their home towns and taken to momentous national and international events, signifying the importance and influence of the universities they represented. When the religious allegiance of Europe to rival popes was debated at the Council of Constance (1414–18) before kings, princes, cardinals and bishops, universities including Heidelberg sent their own delegates attended by their maces to visibly represent their authority.

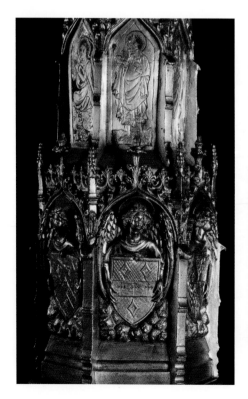 

In commissioning maces the Faculty of Arts and, later in the 15th century, the Faculty of Canon Law and the College of St Salvator in the University of St Andrews were publicly proclaiming their status and importance, and asserting the rights and authority of the new Scottish university as an institution equal to the older universities in Europe. The maces of the University of St Andrews have been used in ceremonies since their creation, as they still are at graduation and other events today.

The **Mace of the Faculty of Arts** was probably made in Paris. It had arrived in St Andrews by December 1419. It has a three-tiered hexagonal head in the Gothic style. It is finely crafted in silver and partially gilded. The highest tier takes the form of a lantern tower with traceried windows. On the middle tier images of popular saints are engraved on silver panels once plated with enamel. St Andrew naturally features. Also represented are St Leonard, St Michael the Archangel, St Margaret of Antioch, St John the Baptist and the Virgin Mary holding the infant Christ.

Below these, angels rise from silver clouds. They hold shields with the heraldry of Scotland; Bishop Henry Wardlaw (founder of the University); Alexander Stewart, 14th Earl of Mar; Archibald, 5th Earl of Douglas; Robert Stewart, 1st Duke of Albany; and (replacing an original shield) Archbishop Spottiswoode, Chancellor 1615–39. Mar, Douglas and Albany were politically prominent in Scotland in the early 15th century, with Albany serving as Regent of Scotland during the captivity of King James I in England.

The **Mace of the Faculty of Canon Law** was created about 1450. It is based on the Arts Mace, and may have been made in Scotland. Figures of St Andrew, the Holy Trinity, the Virgin and Child, St Peter, St John the Baptist and St Kentigern or St Mungo are engraved in silver panels on the mace head.

The **Mace of St Salvator's College** is widely acknowledged to be among the very finest surviving pieces of medieval metalwork. It was commissioned by Bishop James Kennedy for the College of St Salvator, which he had founded in 1450. It was made in Paris in 1461 by the goldsmith Johne Maiel.

The design of the mace is intricate and complex. The head takes the form of an open shrine, containing at its centre the figure of St Salvator, Christ the Holy Saviour, on a globe representing the world. He bears the wounds of the crucifixion. Three angels carry three emblems of the Passion of Christ: the pillar, cross and spear. Below these are three dungeon entrances, each containing a chained wild man with shields representing the see of St Andrews, Bishop Kennedy and St Salvator's College. The figures of a king, a bishop and possibly a merchant probably represent the Three Estates of medieval society.

Detail of the Mace of the Faculty of Arts (far left)

Detail of the Mace of the Faculty of Canon Law (left)

Angels and scholars on the upper knop of the Mace of St Salvator's College (above)

33

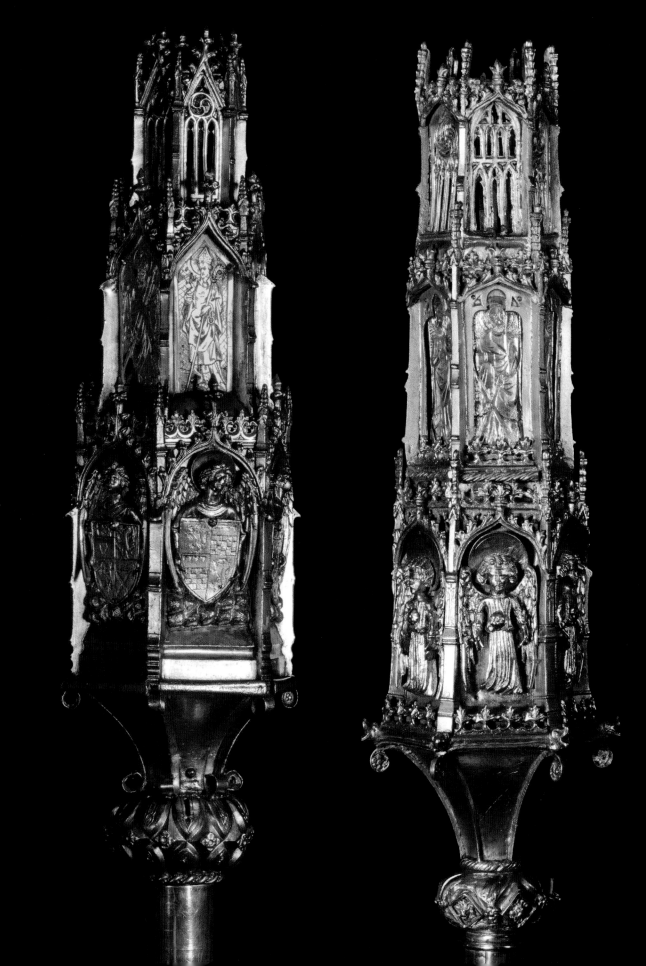

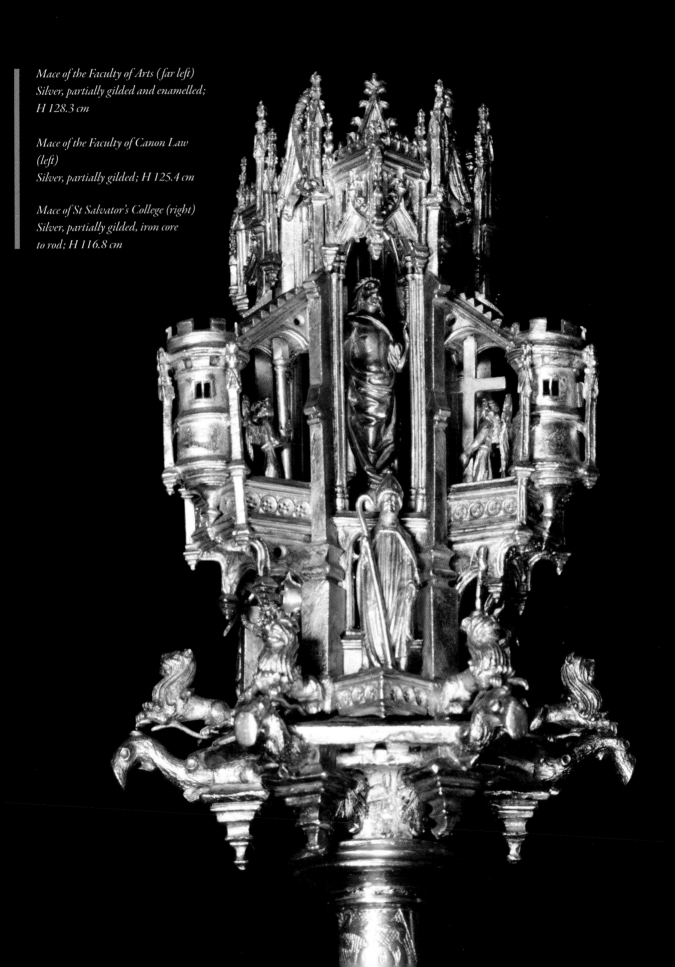

Mace of the Faculty of Arts (far left)
Silver, partially gilded and enamelled;
H 128.3 cm

Mace of the Faculty of Canon Law
(left)
Silver, partially gilded; H 125.4 cm

Mace of St Salvator's College (right)
Silver, partially gilded, iron core
to rod; H 116.8 cm

Forbidden Pleasures
Group of caich balls, 18th or early 19th century

Although approved sports, such as archery, were permitted and even encouraged by the University authorities, certain games were strictly forbidden. The medieval statutes of St Leonard's College restricted the time allowed to students for exercise to just once a week, when 'honest games' might be played on the links. The playing of 'dishonest games', such as football, could be punished with expulsion. The diary of James Melville, a student at St Leonard's in the 1570s, records that his father provided him with bows and arrows for archery, and a golf club and balls, but 'nocht a purss for Catchpull and Tavern' – no money for the game of caich, or for drinking in taverns, both shady activities for a young man to be involved in.

Caich was a popular game among young Scots from the medieval period up to the 19th century. It was an early form of games such as handball and racket sports like squash. It required a wall, a hard flat surface in front of it, and a ball that bounced. Two individuals or teams played against each other, competing to strike the ball with the hand against the wall in a rally. Caich was liable to cause broken windows and other damage. Betting was common, as the refusal of Melville's father to provide money for caich implies. Caich was severely frowned upon throughout the centuries by the University authorities, to the dismay of energetic students. The poet Robert Fergusson, who studied at St Andrews in the 1760s, described how David Gregory, Professor of Mathematics would chase away those hitting balls ('skelpin' at the ba''):

> Sae weel's he'd fley the students a'
> Whan they war skelpin' at the ba',
> They took leg bail and ran awa',
> Wi' pith and speed

This group of caich balls, which textile analysis has dated to the 18th or early 19th centuries, was discovered in the tower of St Salvator's Chapel in 1954. The balls may have been hidden there, or confiscated by an irate master. They are at various stages of construction, providing a unique insight into how they were created. Corks have been tightly wrapped in woollen yarn, and then covered in a leather outer-casing. Such balls were perishable, and very few survive.

Group of caich balls
Leather, wool, flax thread, cork
Diameter of largest ball: 7cm
HC836

Gods and Goddesses

Stone stele depicting Shiva and Parvati, 11th century
Indian painting on glass, mid-19th century

Throughout the 19th century, many graduates and friends of the University worked in British-ruled India. Some of these collected objects which they presented to the joint Museum of the University and the Literary and Philosophical Society of St Andrews, founded in 1838.

Among these donations was a series of ten paintings on glass of Hindu deities, made in Southern India, possibly Tanjore. The work illustrated here shows Gaja Lakshmi, the goddess of wealth and prosperity, attended by elephants. Because of their fragility and their religious subject matter, few such paintings were sent to Britain by expatriates. These paintings were presented to the Museum by Reverend A. Clifford Bell, who was born in Kennoway, Fife in 1832 and educated at the University. From 1860 to 1874 he was Chaplain of St Andrews Church, Madras, possibly acquiring the works at this time.

This stele, or monumental stone, from eastern India or Bengal depicts the Hindu god Shiva and his consort Parvati. It dates from around the 11th century and is made of black chlorite. It was collected in Bengal and presented to the Museum by Reverend James Paterson, a missionary educated in St Andrews, in November 1839.

Shiva and Parvati are seated in *lalitsana*, the position of royal ease, on a lotus base. Below are their vehicles, Shiva's bull Nandi and Parvati's lion, flanked by devotees. The

central, dancing figure is Camunda, a terrifying manifestation of the Mother Goddess Devi. Parvati's mirror is intended to reflect the divine beauty and magnificence of her Lord Shiva.

The stele is supposedly associated with the invention of the gutta percha (rubber) golf ball, which replaced the feathery ball and revolutionised the game of golf. An article in *Golf Illustrated*, 24 January 1902, claimed that in April 1845 a ball was made from the gutta percha in which the stele had been packed for transportation. This rather romantic tale is doubted by several authorities.

Stele depicting Shiva and Parvati (right)
Black chlorite; 88.0 × 43.0 × 34.0 cm
ET26

Painting of Gaja Lakshmi (left)
Paint and gold leaf on glass; 35.3 × 30.0 cm
ET25(6)

Fossilised Fishes

Fish of the species *Holoptychius flemingi*, late Devonian period, excavated at Dura Den

During the mid-19th century, Dura Den, to the west of St Andrews, became one of the most important sites for palaeontology – the study of fossils – in the world. Fossil fish were first found there in 1827, and further specimens were discovered in 1836 by stonemasons working on a mill. The discoveries at Dura Den excited much interest, with various excavations in the 19th century uncovering several species that were new to science. Their extraordinary preservation allowed detailed research and accurate anatomical reconstructions. The fish were examined by several prominent scientists, including the renowned geologists Charles Lyell and Louis Agassiz. Their bone structures fuelled the debate on evolution.

The fish most commonly found at Dura Den is *Holoptychius*, which thrived in the late Devonian period, from 450 to 390 million years ago. *Holoptychius* are lobe-finned fish (Sarcopterygii), with fins located on small stumps, or lobes, which held bones. Encouraged by Darwin's theory of evolution by natural selection, 19th-century scientists suggested that these stumps were related to the development of limbs, and that tetrapods (amphibians, reptiles, birds and mammals, including humans) had evolved from primitive fish-like ancestors. It is now recognised that lobe-finned fishes like the extinct *Holoptychius*, and surviving examples such as the lungfishes and coelacanths, share common ancestry with all tetrapods.

This slab contains five fish of the species *Holoptychius flemingi*, named after John Fleming, a prominent zoologist involved in the excavations. The fish found at Dura Den are generally thought to have been freshwater lake dwellers. Their close groupings suggest that they were forced into smaller areas as the pools they were living in dried up.

This humorous sketch captures a geologist's delight at finding a fish. It appears in the Commonplace Book of Roberta McIntosh, sister of William Carmichael McIntosh, the University's Professor of Natural History. The caption identifies the excavator as Ramsay Traquair, the first Keeper of Natural History at the Royal Museum, Edinburgh. In the 19th century, geologists often dressed formally to conduct fieldwork, to reflect the studious and gentlemanly nature of their occupation.

Slab containing Holoptychius flemingi *(right)*
Upper Old Red Sandstone, 30.0 × 21.0 × 8.0 cm

Watercolour sketch in Roberta McIntosh's Commonplace Book, 1860–68 (left)
St Andrews University Library, Special Collections, ms37102/9

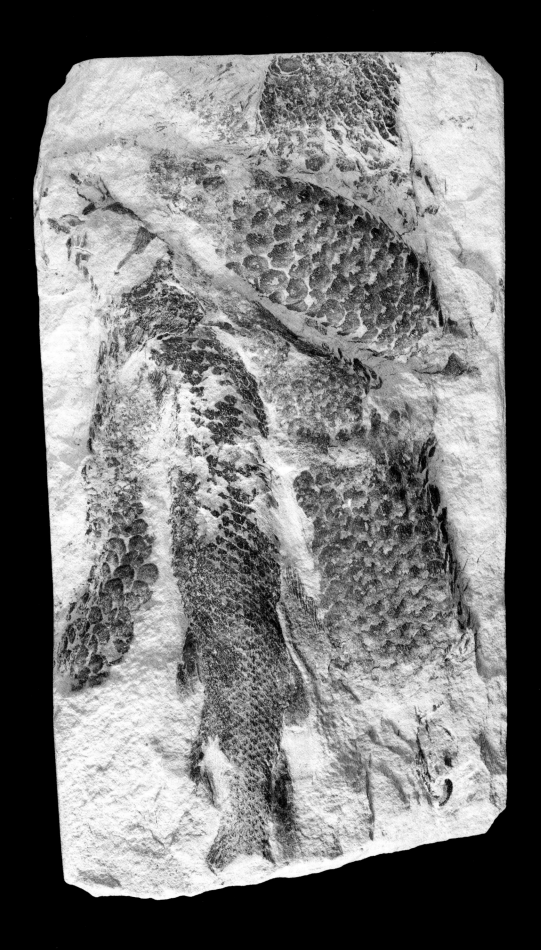

Disrupting Times

'Disruption Brooch'

Memorial window dedicated to Thomas Chalmers, made by Hardman & Co., Birmingham, about 1862

The Disruption of the Church of Scotland was a momentous event in Victorian Scotland, at a time when Christian worship was central to national life and identity. On 18 May 1843, around 200 commissioners refused to take their seats at the annual General Assembly of the Church of Scotland. They walked out of St Andrew's Church, Edinburgh and processed to Tanfield Hall in Canonmills, joined on the way by hundreds of other ministers and watched by crowds of thousands. There they formed the Free Protesting Church of Scotland. 474 ministers (almost 40 per cent of the total) and around half the members of congregations left the Church of Scotland. The ministers were giving up their salaries, churches and homes, the manses, for an uncertain future.

The dispute centred on the Church's authority and the right of the state to intervene in Church affairs, such as the appointment of ministers to parishes. Moderate ministers accepted that the Crown in Parliament had supreme legal power. Evangelicals, led by Thomas Chalmers, asserted that as the Church was under the sole headship of Christ, it could not be subject to the rule of civil law. The Disrupting ministers were compared to the Covenanters of the 17th century, striving to safeguard the religious rights and freedoms of the Scottish people.

Ladies wore silver 'Disruption brooches' to show their support for the Free Church. On the brooches, thistles, representing Scotland, are interspersed with banners bearing key dates in the Church of Scotland's history, symbolically linking the formation of the Free Church with other previous reforms of the Church of Scotland.

Chalmers (1780–1847) became the first Moderator of the General Assembly of the Free Church of Scotland. Under his leadership, the Free Church grew rapidly. By 1847 over 730 places of worship had been built and over 44,000 children attended Free Church Schools.

Chalmers had been a student, and, from 1823 to 1828, Professor of Moral Philosophy in the University of St Andrews. A memorial window to him was installed in St Salvator's Chapel. Made about 1862 by Hardman & Co. of Birmingham, it features Biblical scenes of the Sermon on the Mount, the Last Supper and the Raising of Lazarus. Removed from the Chapel in the 1960s, it is now on display in MUSA.

'Disruption Brooch' (far left)
Silver; 7 cm diameter
HC1997.20

Memorial Window (below)
Glass, lead; 320 × 172 cm
HC816

Model of Practice

Model of a dissected human skull by Tramond of Paris, about 1900

This highly accurate wax model of half a dissected human skull was used to support medical training in the University. Made by the firm Tramond of Paris about 1900, it is part of a collection of around 90 incredibly detailed wax and plaster models from the late 19th century that helped medical students to understand the structure of the different parts of the human body.

The Foundation Bull of 1413 had granted the University the power to examine candidates for Masters degrees and Doctorates in Medicine, as well as Arts, Theology, Canon Law and Civil Law. However, there was no properly organised scheme of practical medical teaching in St Andrews until the 19th century. Occasionally, distinguished physicians happened to be appointed to roles in the University, but this was not for their medical expertise. The eminent royal physician William Schevez, who specialised in diseases of the nervous system, became Archbishop of St Andrews and Chancellor of the University (1478–97). John Wedderburn taught as a professor of philosophy (1620–30) before later being appointed as physician to Charles I. Although a Chair of Medicine was established at St Andrews in 1722, no formal course of instruction was offered. In the 17th and 18th centuries medical degrees were awarded to candidates *in absentia* (without them attending the University), upon receipt of written testimonials from 'eminent practitioners' as to the candidates' suitable character, education and experience. Edward Jenner, who would go on to develop vaccination, was given a degree under this system in 1792.

The introduction of a formal taught medical programme in the University in the mid-19th century meant that instruments, specimens and other tools for instruction were required. Detailed teaching charts and models used in the classroom are now part of the museum collections, and though these historical items are no longer a prime component of instruction, they are still made available to medical students.

Model of dissected skull
Wax; 38.0 × 29.0 × 18.5 cm
MSAM11

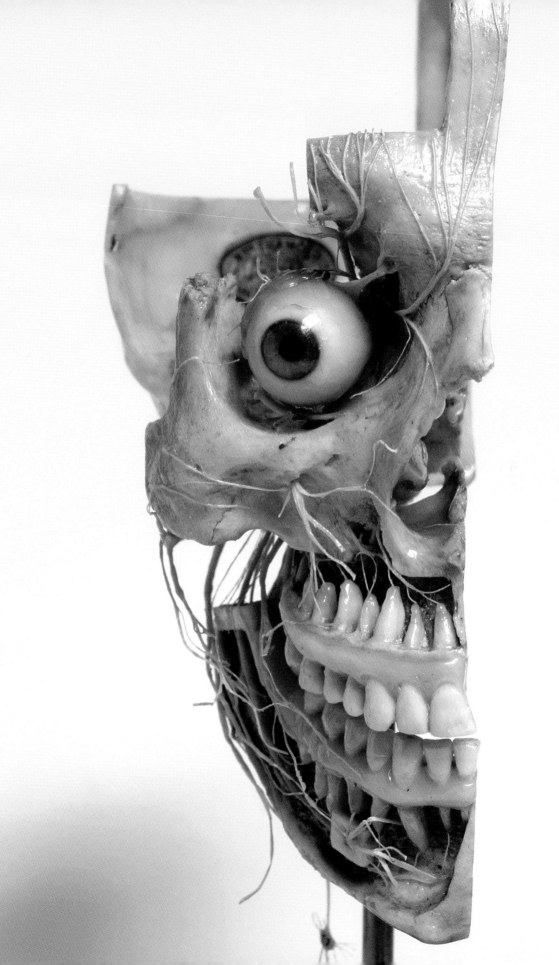

Pioneering Women
L.L.A. badge and sash, early 20th century

Medieval universities were all-male institutions from which women were excluded. At St Leonard's College, statutes issued in 1544 declared that no women were allowed in the college, 'save the common laundress, who must be fifty years at the least', to avoid the distractions of female company in this semi-monastic community. Women continued to be prohibited from studying in universities in Britain until the late 19th century, and were therefore excluded from access to many professions, including law, medicine and academia.

The University of St Andrews played a leading part in developing women's higher education by introducing what became the Lady Literate in Arts (L.L.A.) scheme in 1877. Under this scheme, which continued until 1932, women could gain a higher diploma from

St Andrews by correspondence or 'distance learning', sitting examinations in local centres throughout Britain and, later, overseas. Thousands did so. For conservative Victorian families, this alleviated concerns about daughters living away from home and studying in mixed classes in university towns. Women achieving the L.L.A. diploma were entitled to wear an L.L.A. badge and sash.

Access to higher education for women had been hotly debated in St Andrews for some time before this. In 1862 Elizabeth Garrett, who was to become Britain's first female medical doctor, was allowed to matriculate in St Andrews. However, although she was supported by several of the professors, her enrolment was ultimately declared illegal by the University Senate. An Act of Parliament in 1889 finally allowed the Scottish universities to admit female students to degree courses, and in 1892 nineteen women began at St Andrews. This photograph shows a group of women students in 1896, the year that St Andrews opened Scotland's first university hall of residence for female students, University Hall. By 1912 University Hall provided accommodation for about 70 women, approximately one-fifth of the total student population in St Andrews.

Today, around half of St Andrews students are female and all the halls of residence are mixed. The first female Principal and Vice-Chancellor of the University, Professor Louise Richardson, was appointed in 2009.

L.L.A. badge and sash (above)
Silver and fabric; badge 5.9 × 3.8 cm
HC629

Photograph of group of women students, 1896 (left)
St Andrews University Library,
Special Collections, Ph-Group-1896-4a

Evolutionary Theory
Resplendent Quetzal (*Pharomachrus mocinno*)

This striking quetzal, with its magnificent tail feathers, comes from the collections of the eminent 19th-century naturalist Alfred Russel Wallace. Although his fame has been eclipsed by that of Charles Darwin, Wallace is jointly credited, with Darwin, for the theory of evolution by natural selection.

Darwin first began to privately sketch out his theory of evolution about 1842. He realised that all organisms compete for resources, such as food and good habitats, and that those that have some innate advantage would be more likely to thrive and breed and pass that advantage on to their offspring, gradually leading to changes that would result in the generation of new species. He did not publish his work, knowing how controversial it would be, as it implicitly challenged religious notions of the divine and unchanging order of the world.

In 1858 Alfred Russel Wallace, a young English naturalist working in Indonesia, sent Darwin a draft of his own paper 'On the Tendency of Varieties to Depart Indefinitely from the Original Type', which proved to be uncannily similar to Darwin's thoughts. Their ideas were presented as a joint paper at the Linnaean Society in London on 1 July 1858.

The resplendent quetzal (*Pharomachrus mocinno*) was the sacred bird of the ancient Mayas and Incas who prized its long, iridescent tail feathers for dress and decoration. Its range is Central America and northern parts of South America, living in the cloud-forests of Guatemala, Costa Rica, El Salvador, Honduras, Panama, Nicaragua, and Mexico. The male grows two long tail feathers, up to 1m in length, which attract mates. Deforestation and hunting have endangered the quetzal, with fewer than 50,000 thought to remain. The species appears on the International Union for the Conservation of Nature's Red List of threatened species.

The quetzal, and 45 other birds from Wallace's collections, including a Reeves's Pheasant, parrots, riflebirds, hummingbirds and birds of paradise were presented to the Bell Pettigrew Museum by Dr Albert Günther, Keeper of Zoology at the British Museum. Günther was brother-in-law to the Director of the Bell Pettigrew Museum, William Carmichael McIntosh, Professor of Natural History at the University 1882–1917.

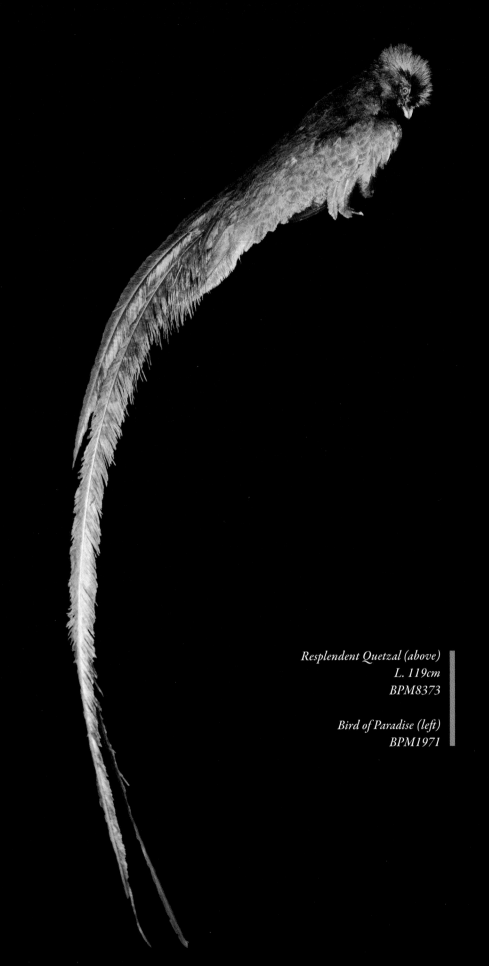

Resplendent Quetzal (above)
L. 119cm
BPM8373

Bird of Paradise (left)
BPM1971

Flights of Fancy

Bronze sculpture of Peter Pan by Sir George Frampton, 1913

The much loved character of Peter Pan was created by the Scottish author and playwright J. M. Barrie. Tales of his adventures in Neverland first appeared in *The Little White Bird*, published in 1902, followed by the stage play *Peter Pan, or The Boy Who Wouldn't Grow Up*, in 1904.

J.M. Barrie was Rector of the University of St Andrews, 1919–22. On 3 May 1922 he gave his celebrated rectorial address 'Courage'. This intensely powerful speech, in part a moving meditation on the loss of young men in the First World War, was delivered before Field Marshal Sir Douglas Haig, Chancellor of the University, in a hall packed with people, some of whom had themselves fought and suffered in the war. On the same day Barrie presented this sculpture of Peter Pan, 'the boy who wouldn't grow up', to the students of University Hall. University Hall had been founded in 1896 as the University's first residence for women students. The sculpture is based on the famous statue of Peter Pan in Kensington Gardens and, like it, was made by Sir George Frampton.

The sculpture in Kensington Gardens, where some of Peter's adventures are based, had been installed overnight by Barrie on the evening of 30 April 1912. He announced the next morning in *The Times* that it was intended as 'a May-day gift' for the children of London. He had not received permission to place it there, however, and though the sculpture is now greatly cherished, at the time questions were asked in the House of Commons about whether an author should be permitted to promote his work by siting a statue of one of his characters in a public park. Barrie was not entirely happy with the appearance of the sculpture, remarking that 'It doesn't show the devil in Peter'. In the work given to the University, Peter Pan also has an innocent, rather than mischievous, appearance.

Sculpture of Peter Pan
Bronze; 60.0 × 23.5 × 29.0 cm
HC801

Tibetan Traditions

Thangka, Tibetan, probably early 19th century

This exquisite *thangka*, or Tibetan painted scroll, is a significant religious and devotional object. It is a *Tshogs Shing*, literally an 'assembly tree', showing the spiritual and doctrinal line of descent in the Gelugpa sect (the 'Yellow Hats') of Buddhism, and the deities and saints revered by that sect. Gelugpa is the form of Tibetan Buddhism associated with the Dalai Lama. Tsongkhapa (1357–1419), founder of the sect, is shown in the upper centre of the *thangka*, surrounded by a white mandorla, or almond-shaped panel.

This type of *thangka* is often found at the entrance to meditation or ceremonial halls, or hanging near shrines or altars. It is used in conjunction with meditation and visualisations on the stages of the path to enlightenment.

*Thangka*s have a complex construction. This *thangka* consists of a gilded painting on canvas sewn into an embroidered silk frame. It has a silk cover, which can be held up by ribbons, and is attached to two poles, one wood and one brass. *Thangka*s are rolled for transport or storage. They are used as visual teaching devices, as well as for devotional

practice. Historically, monks travelling around Tibet to spread Buddhist teachings would carry the rolled scrolls on the backs of yaks. This *thangka* is creased from rolling: the damage has been exaggerated because the silk border is not quite the right size for the painted canvas to which it is attached. It bears stains from butter lamps, which were often placed before scrolls in temples.

This *thangka* was presented to the University in 1951 by Hugh Richardson (1905–2000), a native of St Andrews. A friend of the Dalai Lama, Richardson was a prominent advocate of the cause of Tibetan independence from China. He spent eight years in Tibet as a diplomat between 1936 and 1950, six as Head of Mission in Lhasa first for the British and then the Indian governments. He retired from post shortly before the Chinese invasion in 1951, and wrote extensively on Tibetan history and culture.

Thangka *with silk cover raised (left) and detail (right)*
Oil on canvas, silk, wood, brass, leather; 130.0 × 179.0 cm
ET23

Elements of Chemistry

Chemical glassware, late 18th or early 19th century
Sugar samples, early 20th century

About 1925, several specimens of unusual glassware were discovered in the tower of St Salvator's Chapel. Dating from the late 18th or early 19th centuries, they had been used in the teaching of chemistry, and are thought to have been placed in the tower, which served as a store, for safe-keeping when they came out of use. Such early survivals of chemical glassware are incredibly rare, and these are among the most important in Britain. By its nature, glass is fragile, and when subjected to heat, pressure and other stresses in a busy laboratory, it is easily damaged or destroyed.

Teaching of chemistry began in the University in 1811, when Robert Briggs was appointed to lecture in chemistry and chemical pharmacy. To support his work, the considerable sum of £225.19s.6d was spent on acquiring the apparatus of Dr Thomas Thomson, formerly a private lecturer in chemistry in Edinburgh and later Professor of Chemistry at Glasgow University. Chemical glassware, probably including that found in the tower, is listed on the detailed invoice.

By the first quarter of the 20th century the chemistry department had become a world leader in carbohydrate research. One element of this was the investigation of the structure of sugars, begun by Thomas Purdie, Professor of Chemistry 1885–1909, and continued by his successor, Professor James Colquhoun Irvine (1909–20), later Principal of the University. By the use of chemical reagents, Irvine unravelled the structure of a

number of sugar molecules and confirmed the existence of rings of atoms. He discovered several new sugars, and also made chemical derivatives of sugars as part of the investigation of molecular structures. Around 900 sugar samples are held in the museum collections. Ultimately, Irvine's work on rings of atoms was to have important consequences in the field of biology, informing developments such as the understanding of the structure of DNA.

Chemical glassware (above)
Glass, various sizes. CH15 (left in photo) 23.0 × 51.5 × 35.4 cm
CH15, CH14, CH6 (left to right)

Sugar samples (left)
Various sizes. Largest shown 12.9 × 2.1 cm
CH3

Fine Apparel

Gauntlet gloves of Sir Henry Wardlaw, early 17th century

By tradition, this exquisitely embroidered pair of gauntlet gloves is said to have been presented to Sir Henry Wardlaw of Pitreavie (1565–1637) by Charles I. With their beautiful, eye-catching design and shimmering colours in rich silks, they were created for decorative display, not practical use. The gloves have slender, tapering fingers, too narrow for most adults. Instead of being worn on the hands, decorated gloves were usually either carried or displayed in the hat or the belt, where they could be seen clearly. They were a fashionable, luxurious accessory that indicated the high status of their owner.

Sir Henry served both Charles I and his father James VI of Scotland and I of England. In 1602, he was appointed Chamberlain to James's queen, Anne of Denmark. When James succeeded to the English throne after the death of Elizabeth I in 1603 and departed for England with much of the Scottish court, Wardlaw remained in Scotland and was placed in charge of the royal palace at Dunfermline. He was knighted in 1613. Charles I inherited the English and Scottish thrones from his father in 1625. When he travelled to Scotland in 1633 for the first time since his childhood, for his Scottish coronation, Sir Henry was charged with preparing Dunfermline Palace for the royal visit.

Stylistically, the gloves date from 1610–35. They are made of white leather with gauntlet cuffs of ivory satin finely embroidered with silks, gilt purl coils, threads wrapped with silver strip and hundreds of tiny seed pearls to create an ornately textured surface. The gloves are decorated with motifs of fountains with water spouts, goldfish, flowers and vibrant butterflies or dragonflies. The stylised castle building may be intended to represent Dunfermline Palace. The emblem of a star over the fountains is drawn from the Wardlaw coat of arms.

The gloves passed down through the Wardlaw family before being presented to the University in 2001 together with a copy of the Geneva Bible. Although the royal connection cannot be absolutely proven, for a letter from Charles I once held with the gloves had been lost by the 19th century, the rich design speaks powerfully of the conspicuous display of wealth and status in the 17th century.

Gauntlet gloves (right) and detail (left)
Leather, satin, silk, gilt, seed pearls, lace; 37.0 × 19.5 cm
HC2001.15

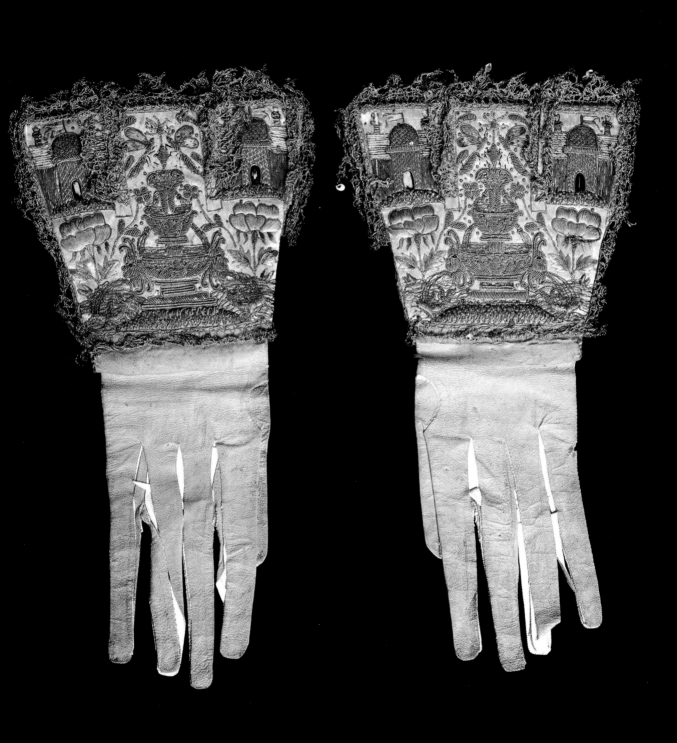

Recording Scotland

Red Row, Limekilns by Alan Ian Ronald, 1942
Ceres, Fife by Samuel Peploe, before 1935

The Recording Britain scheme was established during the first year of the Second World War (1939–45), as an artistic project to create a pictorial record of Britain. It was founded amid fears of various threats to the traditional and familiar scenes of the British Isles. These ranged from enemy action, such as aerial bombardment, to the more general impact of growing urbanisation, industry, motor transport and other aspects of modern life and progress. The scheme also aimed to provide financial support for artists struggling during the war.

Artists were instructed to feature 'views, places and sites likely to be spoiled or destroyed in the future by building encroachments and other causes'.

Recording Britain focused on England and Wales, particularly the southern counties. Recording Scotland was established in 1942, as an extension of the scheme, and, like it, was funded by the Pilgrim Trust. It was administered by a separate Scottish committee, chaired by Sir James Irvine, Principal of the University of St Andrews. The Scottish committee did not issue commissions to artists, as occurred with Recording Britain. Instead they invited artists to submit existing works for consideration, and also bought from dealers and from the Annual Exhibition of the Royal Society of Painters in Water Colours. This meant that they were able to select carefully from the many pictures

Ceres, Fife (above)
Oil on board; 38.0 × 29.0 cm
HC86

Red Row, Limekilns (right)
Watercolour on paper; 37.2 × 45.8 cm
HC106

offered to them, to develop a collection broadly representative of the varied Scottish regions. Works from earlier in the 20th century were sometimes purchased, such *Ceres, Fife* by Samuel Peploe. By the end of the project, the collection contained 145 artworks by 47 artists.

Recording Scotland provides an important illustrative record of a diverse range of Scottish scenes. Artworks depict castles, churches and watermills, village streets, highland cottages and cityscapes of Edinburgh and Glasgow. Scotland's long agricultural, economic and industrial heritage is captured in views ranging from ploughing near Cromarty Firth to the lime works at Charlestown, fishing ports and the industrial infrastructure of the Clyde docks.

While the Recording Britain collection of 1549 works is held by the Victoria and Albert Museum, London, the Recording Scotland collection was presented to the University of St Andrews in 1952, in tribute to the late Principal Irvine.

Cypriot Connections

'Plank idol', 2300–1650 BC

Lamp stand or incense burner, about 800 BC

This 'plank idol' was made in Cyprus in the Early or Middle Cypriot Bronze Age (2300–1650 BC). The name 'plank idol' comes from the flat, generally rectangular, plank-like shape of such pieces. It has stylised facial features and arms, with a halo-like projection over the head. It is made of terracotta, in a style known as White Painted ware, with horizontal red markings. Archaeologists are not certain of the exact function of such pieces. Many 'plank idols' have been found in tombs and seem to have played a role in burial rituals, perhaps as companions for the dead. Unlike this piece, figurines are often female in shape and carry a child. These may have been intended as fertility symbols.

Cyprus is located in the north-eastern area of the Mediterranean Sea. Its position, long history of human occupation, and exposure to the influences of diverse civilisations, from Egyptian and Persian to Greek, Phoenician and Roman, through immigration, occupation and trade, make the island a fertile source for archaeology and the study of ancient and early modern cultures.

The University holds a collection of around 190 Cypriot artefacts, presented by Mrs Margaret Bridges, which illustrate the varied material culture of the island. These range from Bronze Age and Byzantine pottery to clay figurines of humans and animals, jewellery and Roman lamps. Among them is this bronze lamp stand or incense burner, of a type thought to have been made by Phoenician artisans living in Cyprus about the 6th century BC. The lamp rested on the ring at the top. The column is decorated with flowers.

Plank idol (right)
Clay; 15.0 × 6.0 cm
HC1994.3(65)

Lamp stand or incense burner (left)
Bronze; H 33.2 cm
HC1994.3(164)

Contemporary Collecting

Match head: Buddha in yellow, by David Mach, 2007

The Scottish artist David Mach creates artworks and sculptural installations out of mass-produced everyday objects, such as car tyres, wire coat-hangers, matchsticks and magazines. His work sometimes addresses topical or political themes, such as *Polaris*, a life-size replica of a Polaris submarine made out of car tyres, installed outside the Royal Festival Hall in London in 1983 to provoke discussion about the nuclear arms race. Mach's use of ordinary materials to create striking and powerful art challenges us to look afresh at both the subjects his art addresses and the everyday products it employs.

This sculpture of the head of the Buddha has been created from matchsticks, with the coloured tips of the match heads aligned to construct the patterned surface of the face. It is part of a series of human and animalistic heads composed from matchsticks that Mach has produced since 1982. Mach sometimes ignites the match head sculptures, which burst into uncontrollable flames that die down to reveal a charred and transfigured piece. The head of Robert Burns was set alight in 2009 to launch StAnza, Scotland's International Poetry Festival held in St Andrews, and mark the 250th anniversary of the poet's birth. This vivid performance art is an act of creation, not destruction, transforming a carefully constructed object into a new and changed form.

Match head: Buddha in yellow is part of the Harry and Margery Boswell Art Collection at the University of St Andrews. The collection was established and endowed by the Boswell family in 1996, with subsequent generous donations, to enable the University to make annual purchases of notable Scottish art. To date, collecting has focused primarily on the fields of contemporary and mid- to late 20th-century Scottish paintings, prints, sculptures and photographs, which had previously been something of a gap in the collections. The artists represented include the leading figures of Robin Philipson, Alan Davie, Calum Colvin, John Bellany, Steven Campbell, Alison Watt, Will Maclean and Adrian Wiszniewski, and from earlier in the 20th century J.D. Fergusson and William McCance. The Boswell Collection supports teaching and research in Scottish art and culture in the University, particularly within the School of Art History.

Match head: Buddha in yellow
Matchsticks; 25.0 × 22.0 × 15.0 cm
HC2008.3

Index